# THE "DAILY" Source Book

*By*
**Heidi Heiks**

**TEACH Services, Inc.**
PUBLISHING
www.TEACHServices.com • (800) 367-1844

**PRINTED IN
THE UNITED STATES OF AMERICA**

World rights reserved. This book or any portion thereof may not be copied or reproduced in any form or manner whatever, except as provided by law, without the written permission of the publisher, except by a reviewer who may quote brief passages in a review. The author assumes full responsibility for the accuracy of all facts and quotations as cited in this book.

This book was written to provide accurate and authoriative information in regard to the subject matter covered. It is sold with the understanding that the publisher is not engaged in giving legal, accounting, medical or other professional advice. If legal advice or other professional expert assistance is required, the reader should seek a competent professional person.

Copyright © 2008 TEACH Services, Inc.
ISBN-13: 978-1-57258-558-4
ISBN-10: 1-57258-558-7
Library of Congress Control Number: 2008907793

# FOREWORD

The problem of the interpretation of the *daily* or "continual" (Hebrew *tamid*) which Heidi Heiks addresses in this excellent study has long been a point of contention among Seventh-day Adventist interpreters. What has been called the "old view" of the *daily* was held by most writers in the church through the 19th century. Then around the turn of the century, the so-called "new view" of the *daily* was proposed by leaders like W. C. White, A. G. Daniels, L. R. Conradi and W. W. Prescott. The debate at that time was particularly heated and both sides appealed to Ellen G. White to decide the issue. She left it unsettled by stating that she had no special light on the subject.

As Heiks points out from his review of the earlier commentary literature, the "new view" of the *daily* was actually older than the so-called "old view" of the *daily*. He cites commentaries all the way back to the Reformation of the 16th century, which show that the *daily* during that era was understood to be the true worship of God in the gospel that was cast down to the earth and disfigured by man. Early SDA interpreters, though, followed William Miller in holding that the *daily* was paganism that was taken out of the way to make for the rise of the religious phase of Rome.

It is instructive to see, as Heiks has detailed, how Miller came to that view. It was not on the basis of linguistics or context in Daniel, but by superimposing 2 Thessalonians 2 upon the text of Daniel, as a quote from Miller's writing shows. This view went essentially unchallenged until the shift mentioned above that began about 1900. The "new view" of the daily probably is more widely held today, but there still are those who advocate the "old view," sometimes quite vigorously.

Heiks has put Miller's error in bold relief. Since he applied Daniel 8:14 to the cleansing of this world and the church by fire at the Second Advent, he of necessity had to place the *tamid* or *daily* here in this world, also.

Restudy of the sanctuary in this verse and elsewhere in Daniel 8 has pointed to the heavenly sanctuary, where Jesus ministers for us in the sanctuary in question. That should place the *daily* in the context of the heavenly sanctuary, as well.

In the Hebrew of the Old Testament the word *tamid* is used as an adverb, which modifies a verbal motion, to point out that the action goes on regularly, consistently or continually—"daily" at regular, repeated intervals. As such, it is used almost thirty times in connection with the tabernacle in the wilderness and the temple in Jerusalem. In these instances, it is always used with some action the priest carried out in its courtyard or in the holy place. It is never used of any object or action in the most holy place, because the priest went in there only once a year. Nor is it ever used of pagan worship or the use of idols. It is found connected with the morning and evening burnt offering on the altar in the sanctuary courtyard, and it is found in connection with attending to the lamps of the menorah, burning incense on the altar of incense and even with the changing of the loaves of bread on the table of showbread, the latter act being done every week on Sabbath morning.

The question, then, is what single word or phrase can encompass all of these regular priestly activities in the sanctuary? Some would like to limit the application of the word *daily* to just the burnt offering in the courtyard, but that would overlook the greater part of those activities. The words in English encompass all of those priestly "ministries" or "ministrations" in the holy place, as well. Thus the "daily" phase of the activity was carried out by the priest in the Holy Place, which was followed once a year by the "yearly" or "annual" ministration in the Most Holy Place. Since these earthly functions were a typological model of what takes place in the heavenly sanctuary, its connection there shows that it belongs to the heavenly mediation and intercession of Christ on behalf of His earthly children.

Let us praise God for the way in which He works out our salvation in this heavenly manner. However, earthly religious powers could not leave well enough alone. They have attempted to turn the attention of mankind away from this true heavenly source of our salvation to earthly substitutions. With the great judgment scene of Daniel 7:9–14 and the reference to it in Daniel 8:14, the truth about this conflict is made plain, but the attacks upon the daily ministry of Christ in heaven will be resolved in the great judgment Day of Atonement.

Brother Heiks has spelled out many aspects of this great truth in his sound linguistic, exegetical, contextual and historical work on these pages.

William H. Shea, Ph.D.
Retired Professor: Old Testament Department
Seminary, Andrews University
Retired Associate: Biblical Research Institute
General Conference of Seventh-day Adventists

## PREFACE

What is the heart of Seventh-day Adventism? Unequivocally, it is found in Daniel 8:9–14: the cleansing of the sanctuary.

> "The correct understanding of the ministration in the heavenly sanctuary is the foundation of our faith." Letter 208, 1906.
>
> "The subject of the sanctuary and the investigative judgment should be clearly understood by the people of God. All need a knowledge for themselves of the position and work of their great High Priest. Otherwise it will be impossible for them to exercise the faith which is essential at this time or to occupy the position which God designs them to fill.
>
> ". . . It is of the utmost importance that all should thoroughly investigate these subjects and be able to give an answer to everyone that asketh them a reason of the hope that is in them." *Great Controversy*, 488–9.

Why does Ellen White put so much emphasis on all needing knowledge for themselves?

> "Every position of truth taken by our people will bear the criticism of the greatest minds; the highest of the world's great men will be brought in contact with truth, and therefore every position we take should be critically examined and tested by the Scriptures. Now we seem to be unnoticed, but this will not always be. Movements are at work to bring us to the front, and if our theories of truth can be picked to pieces by historians or the world's greatest men, it will be done.
>
> "We must individually know for ourselves what is truth, and be prepared to give a reason of the

hope that we have with meekness and fear, not in a proud, boasting self-sufficiency, but with the spirit of Christ. We are nearing the time when we shall stand individually alone to answer for our belief." Letter 6, 1886.

To enhance understanding of the "daily" both scripturally and historically is the purpose of this book, and to prepare all to be able to stand individually and alone in the courtroom to answer for our faith. ". . . A workman that needeth not to be ashamed, rightly dividing the word of truth." 2 Tim. 2:15. Therefore, it is my commitment to you to supply you with all the necessary facts and scripture to fortify your minds so at the end of this study, you will be able to give an answer to anyone that asks, and to do it with confidence. Standing alone before a judge or jury to defend our beliefs is neither the time nor the place to realize that we are confused in our ideas of what we had accepted as truth—to realize we had been building with rotten timbers.

What we here document will be new to some Seventh-day Adventists. It will change the viewpoints of many who have been taught interpretations inconsistent with the facts you are about to read. Please understand that we cannot and do not hold those who took positions different from what is to be presented in a subversive light, for they have based their understanding on what little information they had.

Our subject matter is the "daily," a topic on which our church is unnecessarily divided, as you will soon see. You may ask, "Does it really matter what one believes about the 'daily'? Can this issue ever be truly, finally resolved?" We believe so, and our intention is unity. The information you are about to digest is to be a stepping stone to help bring the unity that Christ prayed for in John 17. We believe that any wedge between brothers—any inconsistency in our beliefs—can and will be exploited by those who wish to undermine the confidence we have in our faith. The more we are fortified by the truth, the more unshakeable and capable will be our testimony when we are called to stand alone before kings and counselors.

In the past, various church leaders have offered a cash reward to any claimant of Sunday as the "Christian Sabbath" who can produce a Bible text proving it was God's will that such a change from the seventh day Sabbath be made. The standing offer was made to make people think and study for themselves. The reward money has never been collected, and a similar offer is here presented: $1000 cash to any "first finder" who can produce even one Bible text from the Authorized Version that states that the "daily" is paganism. Or if anyone can refute the biblical information herein presented on the "daily"—directly disputing this information or the conclusions here put forth with substantive, authoritative biblical evidence—let him do so without delay, that we may "come together" and strive for the unity our Saviour longed for among us.

We also offer a $1000 "first-finder's" reward for substantive proof from the Authorized Version that the "daily" is a pagan desolating power, or for supported evidence from the Authorized Version that the "transgression of desolation" is an anti-God desolating power in the form of the papacy. Such proof, if forthcoming, will be published on my website: www.thesourcehh.org. The reward money can be collected from there, as well. The motivation for this book, the overall goal in mind, is a united front in the face of the enemy. To that end is my sincere prayer.

Heidi Heiks
Author: *508 538 1798 1843 Source Book (Preliminary)*
Former international Christian editor and speaker
Former college educator
Former speaker: *The People of the Book* radio program

## ACKNOWLEDGMENTS

I want to thank Tim Poirier and Larry Crews of the White Estate for all their willing assistance in helping me to pull all this together, and to Tim, in particular, for granting me the right to publish this documentation along with LeRoy Froom's *The Historical Setting and Background of the Term "Daily."* Also, my appreciation goes to Bert Haloviak, Director of Archives and Statistics of the General Conference, for his willingness for me to use selec-tive material that I requested on this topic from his department. I also want to thank Marcus Frey at the Ellen G. White vault at Andrews University for all of his kind and courteous help. And my many thanks go to copyeditor Jean Handwerk for her ceaseless input and suggestions that made this manuscript what it is. My utmost appreciation goes to my wife Robin for her encouragement and admirable patience to see this to completion.

Heidi Heiks

## CONTENTS

Foreword ............................................................. iii
Preface ................................................................ vii
Acknowledgments ............................................... xi

1. Biblical Definition of the "Daily" ........................ 1
2. "New" and "Old" Views Clarified ..................... 13
3. Exposition of Early Writings, 74–76 ................. 29
4. Word Studies, World History, and the
   Fall of Paganism ............................................. 57
5. AD 508: Christ's Ministry "Taken Away" ......... 87
6. AD 538: Sunday Laws Fulfill Prophecy ......... 103
7. Two Desolating Powers? .............................. 125
8. The "Treading Down" of the Sanctuary
   and Host ...................................................... 143
9. Daniells and Prescott Issues ......................... 157
10. The Sanctuary is the Lord's ......................... 179
11. Paganism's Ever-Changing Views ............... 195
12. Ministry View Integral to
    Adventism's Message ................................. 215

# 1

## BIBLICAL DEFINITION OF THE "DAILY"

How shall we begin? We believe that all doctrine must first be derived from the scriptures alone. We will then look at the writings of Ellen White, and next review what was actually taught and believed by Adventism's founding fathers. We will document every piece of information we present from the personal and private letters of the leading brethren from the 1830s to beyond the death of Ellen G. White. These letters were their correspondence to one another related to the ongoing discussion of the "daily." Finally, we will investigate history's contribution to our study of the "daily."

Some may be asking, "Why should Seventh-day Adventists even be looking at this topic in this late hour?" There are actually many reasons, as we will soon illustrate. The first and foremost one is that God has given His final instruction to Ellen White regarding our duty and responsibility concerning this topic. Many have assumed that counsel for silence on the matter can be found in the third book of *Selected Messages*, pages 164–168, but that is a false assumption. If one knew the circumstances confronting the church at that time, it would be seen as only natural that Ellen White would caution the church in those pages with the instruction,

> "Under present conditions, silence is eloquence."

Likewise, in that time period she wrote,

> "Let not 'the daily,' or any other subject that will arouse controversy among brethren, be brought in at this time." Another admonition was spelled out this way: "As a result of the way this subject has been handled by men on both sides of the question, controversy has arisen and confusion has resulted."

However, God gave additional counsel through Mrs. White of which many are unaware. It was not intended that we never agree on the "daily." It was not meant that there would be no end to this controversy on the "daily" which divides us. In fact, we read in inspired counsel that we are to resolve this matter among us.

It is in the following letter that we will find the last clear directives from heaven to God's people regarding our duty and response to this subject. Let us fully comprehend our instruction:

> "MR No. 1470 - Doctrines to Be Investigated; Unity to Be Sought (Written May 24, 1910, from Sanitarium, California, to Elder and Mrs. S. N. Haskell.)
>
> "I have been waiting for the time when there should be an investigation of the doctrines that Brother Daniells and others have been advocating. When is this to be?
>
> "If Elder Daniells thinks that some of the interpretations of Scripture that have been held in the past are not correct, our brethren should listen to his reasons, and give candid consideration to his views. All should examine closely their own standing, and by a thorough knowledge of the principles of our faith, be prepared to vindicate the truth.
>
> "We must not be inconsistent in this matter. God requires clean hearts, pure minds, and an intelligent belief in the truth. 'Faith is the substance of things hoped for, the evidence of things not seen.' At present there is not that unity that should exist among our brethren, and the Lord says, 'Come together.' This should be done as soon as possible, for we have no time to lose.
>
> "Is not the present a favorable time for you and others of our ministering brethren in this conference to meet with Elder Daniells for a thorough examination of the points of faith

regarding which there are different views? [Isaiah 11:1-16; 12:1-6, quoted.]

"I am directed to write these Scriptures for the consideration of those who shall assemble for the purpose of blending together under the guidance of the Holy Spirit. 'Bind up the testimony, seal the law among My disciples.' A special work now rests upon us of solemnly investigating these matters, and in the name of the Lord to unify."–Letter 50, 1910; *Manuscript Releases*, 20:223. [Tim Poirer of the White Estate has confirmed that this letter is in reference to the "daily."]

The letter was plain in its intention and the counsel was clear. Seventh-day Adventists were to study the issue out and ***unify!*** But did they?

The answer can be found in Arthur White's six-page article entitled "Concerning Elder A. G. Daniells," published December 4, 1953, in file no. DF 201-b, pg. 2. We quote:

"What Actually Took Place

"On May 24, 1910, Mrs. E. G. White called Elder W. C. White to her room and asked what was being done in regard to the teaching of the new and old views of the 'daily.' She asked why those who were leading out in these discussions did not get together and study the matter unitedly, and she expressed regret that such a meeting had not been held. On that same day she dispatched a letter to Elder S. N. Haskell, and directed that copies should be sent to Elders Loughborough, Irwin, and Daniells. In this she made an appeal for the brethren who were then on the Pacific Coast, including those named above and also Elder Salisbury to come together in 'examination of the points of faith regarding which there are different views.' The meeting failed to materialize."

This failure on the part of early Adventists does not change the directive given to God's people. The Lord *still* says,

> "'Come together.' This should be done as soon as possible, for we have no time to lose." Letter 50, 1910; *Manuscript Releases*, 20:223.

Assured by this conclusive documentation then, that our study is in obedience to divine will, let us begin.

But how shall we handle the same sensitive subject at this present time? Graciously, our lovingly heavenly Father never leaves His children without counsel and instruction:

> "Nothing frightens me more than to see the spirit of variance manifested by our brethren. We are on dangerous ground when we cannot meet together like Christians, and courteously examine controverted points. I feel like fleeing from the place lest I receive the mold of those who cannot candidly investigate the doctrines of the Bible. Those who cannot impartially examine the evidences of position that differs from theirs, are not fit to teach in any department of God's cause.
> 
> "When the Spirit of God rests upon you, there will be no feeling of envy or jealousy in examining another position; there will be no spirit of accusation and criticism, such as Satan inspired in the hearts of the Jewish leaders against Christ You must have the divine mold before you can discern the sacred claims of the truth. Unless the teacher is a learner in the school of Christ, he is not fitted to teach others."
>
> "If there is a point of truth that you do not understand, upon which you do not agree, investigate, compare scripture with scripture.
>
> "Would it not be well for us to go under the fig tree to plead with God as to what is truth?

> "God wants us to depend upon him, and not upon man. He desires us to have a new heart; he would give us revealing of light from the throne of God. We should wrestle with every difficulty, but when some controverted point is presented, are you to go to man to find out his opinion, and then shape your conclusion from his?—No, go to God.
>
> "When a message is presented to God's people, they should not rise up in opposition to it; they should go to the Bible, comparing it with the law and the testimony, and if it does not bear this test, it is not true." *Review and Herald*, February 18, 1890.

With that inspired counsel before us, let us resolve to calmly and intelligently pursue our topic under consideration. "Let not your faith stand in the wisdom of men, but in the power of God." 1 Cor. 2:5. Ellen White simplifies this Biblical truth with the following:

> "Let all who accept human authority, the customs of the church, or the traditions of the fathers, take heed to the warning conveyed in the words of Christ, 'In vain they do worship Me, teaching for doctrines the commandments of men.'" *Desire of Ages*, 398.
>
> "We are not to make a study as to what are the opinions of men, what are the traditions of the Fathers, or what is the popular faith. We cannot trust to the voice of the multitude, or follow the world in an evil course. Our inquiry should be, What hath God said.?
>
> "The duty of studying the Scriptures is not left as an optional matter, on which little depends. The Lord positively enjoins upon every believer the study of his word, that he may have an intelligent faith, built upon the knowledge of the word of truth. He must dig for truth as one who digs for hidden treasure. He must search the Scriptures, comparing scripture with scripture, and thus

fitting himself to become a laborer with God in a more extended work." *Medical Missionary*, May 1, 1892.

"We shall be attacked on every point; we shall be tried to the utmost. We do not want to hold our faith simply because it was handed down to us by our fathers. Such a faith will not stand the terrible test that is before us." *Review and Herald*, April 29, 1884.

Have Seventh-day Adventists been guilty of holding onto the traditions of the fathers above a "thus saith the Lord"? According to Inspiration, we find in the affirmative. Indeed, we have been given a warning and a prediction on this very issue.

So what is our only safe and due course?

"But God will have a people upon the earth to maintain the Bible, and the Bible only, as the standard of all doctrines and the basis of all reforms." *Great Controversy*, 595.

This obviously leaves no room for the traditions of the fathers or the opinions of men. But where does this place the writings of Ellen White? Let us allow her to answer this question.

"The Lord designs to warn you, to reprove, to counsel, through the testimonies given, and to impress your minds with the importance of the truth of His word. The written testimonies are not to give new light, but to impress vividly upon the heart the truths of inspiration already revealed. Man's duty to God and to his fellow man has been distinctly specified in God's word, yet but few of you are obedient to the light given. Additional truth is not brought out; but God has through the Testimonies simplified the great truths already given and in His own chosen way brought them before the people to awaken and impress the mind with them, that all may be left without excuse." *Testimonies,* 5:665.

Here we see that the *Testimonies* were given to impress upon the mind the truthfulness of God's written word. They did not give new light, neither additional light, but, rather, they simplified the great truths already given in His word, that all may be left without excuse.

One of the Biblical tests of a true prophet of God is found in the book of Isaiah.

> Isa. 8:20 "To the law [the first five books of the Old Testament, which includes the ten commandments] and to the testimony [the prophets]: if they speak not according to this word, it is because there is no light in them."

I think all are agreed that Ellen White has to be to be placed under one of two banners. She is either a true prophet proclaiming simplified truths from God's word, or she is a false prophet having no light whatsoever. The former places the divine stamp on her written counsel; the latter makes all of her words suspect. There is no middle ground here. We endorse the former, and we take the position that when Ellen White speaks, it is not her words but God's word simplifying the great truths already given in the Bible.

> "Permit me to express my mind, and yet not my mind, but the word of the Lord." Letter 89, 1899.

For those who would take issue with this, we have the following counsel.

> "I have my work to do, to meet the misconceptions of those who suppose themselves able to say what is testimony from God and what is human production. If those who have done this work continue in this course, satanic agencies will choose for them.

> "Those who have helped souls to feel at liberty to specify what is of God in the Testimonies and what are the uninspired words of Sister White, will find that they were helping the devil in his work of deception
>
> "What reserve power has the Lord with which to reach those who have cast aside His warnings and reproofs, and have accredited the testimonies of the Sapirit of God to no higher source than human wisdom? In the judgment, what can you who have done this, offer to God as an excuse for turning from the evidences He has given you that God was in the work?" *Selected Messages*, 3:70.

We cannot think of one excuse. Seventh-day Adventists have a history which involves significant contributions by Ellen White. If she had "no light" in her, then our church's teachings automatically become suspect, and those who question her prophetic gift logically would not choose to be members of a church with questionable foundations. But true, grounded Seventh-day Adventists have acquainted themselves with the facts, and for them, when the Bible and Spirit of Prophecy speak on any given topic, a harmony is seen. That harmony will be witnessed in our present study, as well, which should end all controversy and contrary views. Thus we submit and acknowledge that the same Holy Spirit that inspired the prophets of old inspired the writings of Ellen White. Both, therefore, will speak and uphold one and the same meaning. So let us now proceed with the purpose of this thesis: to establish, for all time and for the sake of unity, the meaning and significance of the "daily."

Just where, though, should a Bible-believing Christian begin his or her study of the "daily"? There is no answer but one. We first look to the pages of Holy Writ, as Inspiration rightly confirms:

> "All who handle the Word of God are engaged in a most solemn and sacred work; for in their

> research they are to receive light and a correct knowledge that they may give to those who are ignorant. Education is the inculcation of ideas, which are light and truth. Everyone who diligently and patiently searches the Scriptures that he may educate others, entering upon the work correctly and with an honest heart, laying aside his preconceived ideas, whatever they may have been, and his hereditary prejudices at the door of investigation, will gain true knowledge. But it is easy to put a false interpretation on Scripture, placing stress on passages, and assigning to them a meaning, which, at the first investigation, may appear true, but which by further search, will be seen to be false. If the seeker after truth will compare Scripture with Scripture, he will find the key that unlocks the treasure house and gives him a true understanding of the Word of God. Then he will see that his first impressions would not bear investigation, and that continuing to believe them would be mixing falsehood with truth." *Manuscript 4,* 1896.
>
> Isa. 28:10 "For precept must be upon precept, precept upon precept; line upon line, line upon line; here a little, and there a little."

Following the counsel of Inspiration and Isaiah 28:10, let us now turn to Daniel 8:11, where we find the first reference to the "daily." It is in this first usage of the term that we find its definition, theme, and intended context.

> Dan. 8:11 "Yea, he magnified himself even to the prince of the host, and by him the daily sacrifice was taken away, and the place of his sanctuary was cast down."

In the Hebrew of the Old Testament, "daily" is *tamid* or *tamiyd* (#8548 in *Strong's* or Old Testament lexicons). The context of its usage gives certain light as to its meaning. The theme and context in which the "daily" finds its home in the book of Daniel is none other than that of the sanctuary. As we look at the following texts, it will become abundantly clear to the reader that the prophets had one thought in mind and one only: the "daily" was always used in connection with the ministerial work of the priest in the first apartment. Never was the "daily" attributed to the work of the priest in the second apartment, or to anything else, as will be shown in the following biblical verses. In every case, the underlined word, each one written in the context of the sanctuary, has the very same reference number "8548" as does the "daily" in Daniel 8:11 in the Old Testament. Without question, then, the meaning of the "daily" is synonymous with the meaning of these words.

> Ex. 25:30 "And thou shalt set upon the table shewbread before me <u>alway</u>."
>
> Ex. 27:20–21 "And thou shalt command the children of Israel, that they bring thee pure oil olive beaten for the light, to cause the lamp to burn <u>always</u>. In the tabernacle of the congregation without the vail, which is before the testimony, Aaron and his sons shall order it from evening to morning before the LORD: it shall be a statute for ever unto their generations on the behalf of the children of Israel."
>
> Ex. 29:38 "Now this is that which thou shalt offer upon the altar; two lambs of the first year day by day <u>continually</u>."
>
> Ex. 29:42 "This shall be a <u>continual</u> burnt offering throughout your generations at the door of the tabernacle of the congregation before the LORD: where I will meet you, to speak there unto thee."
>
> Ex. 30:8 "And when Aaron lighteth the lamps at even, he shall burn incense upon it, a <u>perpetual</u> incense before the LORD throughout your generations."

Turning now to the book of Hebrews, we find total consistency from the Old Testament prophets to the New:

Heb. 7:3 "Without father, without mother, without descent, having neither beginning of days, nor end of life; but made like unto the Son of God; abideth a priest <u>continually</u>."

Heb. 7:27 "Who needeth not <u>daily</u>, as those high priests, to offer up sacrifice, first for his own sins, and then for the people's: for this he did once, when he offered up himself."

Heb. 9:6 "Now when these things were thus ordained, the priests went <u>always</u> into the first tabernacle, accomplishing the service of God."

Heb. 10:1 "For the law having a shadow of good things to come, and not the very image of the things, can never with those sacrifices which they offered year by year <u>continually</u> make the comers thereunto perfect."

Heb. 10:11 "And every priest standeth <u>daily</u> ministering and offering oftentimes the same sacrifices, which can never take away sins."

Here we see perfect harmony between Old and New Testaments. Let us now inquire if Ellen White is in harmony with the rule of faith:

"After His ascension, our Saviour was to begin His work as our High Priest. Says Paul, 'Christ is not entered into the holy places made with hands, which are the figures of the true; but into heaven itself, now to appear in the presence of God for us.' Hebrews 9:24. As Christ's ministration was to consist of two great divisions, each occupying a period of time and having a distinctive place in the heavenly sanctuary, so the typical ministration consisted of two divisions, the <u>daily</u> and the yearly service, and to each a department of the tabernacle was devoted. As Christ at His ascension appeared in the presence of God to plead His blood in behalf of penitent believers, so the priest in the <u>daily</u> ministration sprinkled the blood of the sacrifice in the holy place in the sinner's behalf." *Patriarch and Prophets*, 357.

"The ministration of the earthly sanctuary consisted of two divisions; the priests ministered <u>daily</u> in the holy place, while once a year the high priest performed a special work of atonement in the most holy, for the cleansing of the sanctuary. <u>Day by day</u> the repentant sinner brought his offering to the door of the tabernacle and, placing his hand upon the victim's head, confessed his sins, thus in figure transferring them from himself to the innocent sacrifice. Such was the work that went on, <u>day by day</u>, throughout the year. The sins of Israel were thus transferred to the sanctuary, and a special work became necessary for their removal." *Great Controversy*, 418.

Once again we see perfect harmony. Those three harmonious sources clearly demonstrate the following principle, stated variously:

Gen. 41:32 "And for that the dream was doubled unto Pharaoh twice; it is because the thing is established by God."
1 Cor. 14:29 "Let the prophets speak two or three, and let the other judge."
2 Cor. 13:1 "This is the third time I am coming to you. In the mouth of two or three witnesses shall every word be established."

From nowhere in the entire Bible has anyone been able to produce even one text that says the "daily" is paganism—*not one!*—despite rewards offered for such evidence. That's because the Bible nowhere endorses that premise. That interpretation is alien to the Bible and to the prophets, and so is its doctrine. With no Biblical support, one does not have a Biblical doctrine and should not advocate it as such. And what other authority could be claimed? Rather, our firm foundation has been strongly established on the Rock by "it is written."

# 2

## "NEW" AND "OLD" VIEWS CLARIFIED

Today we hear the terms "old view" and "new view" of the "daily." By investigating their origins and their implications, we are to learn much. These terms are applied to paganism (the so-called "old view") and Christ's mediation (the so-called "new view"). Both views were held in the Millerite movement prior to 1844, as well as during the decade following the Disappointment, as will be illustrated.

So how did the brethren come to divergent conclusions about the "daily"? In pulling the curtain back to look behind the scenes of history, we will find our answers. Our next step, therefore, is to examine the unbiased historical documentation from 1831 to the death of Ellen White in 1915. Only then will we be able to finally access the facts, forever lay the many so-called discrepancies to rest, and then address *Early Writings*, pages 74–6. Our pledge to you is this: We will introduce only the facts with the necessary documentation. Never once will we advocate a theory of private interpretation, for it has been this very premise and assumption that has brought in the present confusion and disunity.

We shall begin by setting the record straight by separating the myths from the facts. From the centuries of the Protestant Reformation we have historical proof how the "daily" in Daniel 8 was first interpreted and understood by the Lord's Church. The following documentation has been taken from the Ellen G. White vaults in Silver Spring, MD, and Berrien Springs, MI. The titles alone indicate the beliefs of the authors, and the dates reveal the longevity of that consensus.

> "Daily Sacrifice of True Gospel Supplanted by Mass to Saint Worship." Conradus, Alphonsus, *Commentary on the Revelation* (Basle, 1550), 451.

> "Daily Sacrifice Is Preaching of True Gospel." Armsdorf, Nicholas, *Five Prominent Signs of the Coming of the Judgment Day* (Jena, 1554), unpaged.
>
> "Papacy Casts Down True Worship (Daily Sacrifice)." Parker, Thos., *Visions and Prophecies of Daniel Expounded* (London, 1646), 45, 133.
>
> "Daily Sacrifice—Abolished or Disfigured Worship." Fletcher, John W., "A Letter Upon the Prophecies," in 1755 in *Posthumous Pieces*, 3rd ed. (London, 1800), 372.
>
> "Dan. 12:10—Daily Sacrifice is Divine Worship." Wood, Hans, *Revelation of St. John* (London, 1787), 476.
>
> "Daily Sacrifice (Dan.8)—Worship of God in the Church." Mason, Arch., *Two Essays on Daniel's Prophetic Number of 2300 Days* (Newburg, 1820), 1-6.

Thus for nearly three hundred years there was total consistency on the "daily." And, as illustrated in the last chapter, this understanding stood our test of investigation of the scriptures. So where do we look for the origin and interpretation as the "daily" as paganism? William Miller. Miller here explained the basis for his conclusion:

> "I read on and could find no other case in which it [the "daily"] was found, but in Daniel. I then took those words which stood in connection with it, 'take away,' He shall take away the daily, 'from the time the daily shall be taken away,' etc. I read on and, thought I should find no light on the text; finally I came to 2 Thess. 2:7, 8. 'For the mystery of iniquity doth already work, only he who now letteth, will let, until he be taken out of the way, and then shall that wicked be revealed,' etc. And when I had come to that text, O how clear and glorious the truth appeared. There it is! That is 'the daily!' Well now what does Paul mean by 'he who now

letteth,' or hindereth: By 'the man of sin,' and 'the wicked,' popery is meant. Well what is it which hinders popery from being revealed? Why it is paganism; well then 'the daily' must mean paganism."—Miller, quoted in *Signs of the Times*, Nov. 16, 1842, p. 66, col. 3.

Miller's view linking the "daily" to the 666 years was clearly disclosed in his manuscripts in 1831 ("A Few Evidences of the Time of the 2$^{nd}$ Coming of Christ," p. 8, Feb. 15, 1831; and "Art. No. 3" for *Vermont Telegraph*, 1831, both in Advent Source Collection), and in book form in 1836. His position was that the ten–horned beast from the sea (in Rev. 13) was pagan Rome, and the two-horned beast from the earth was the papal image of paganism. Then, as the second or papal beast exercised power for 1260 years (the forty-two months of vs. five), so pagan Rome's period was 666 years, beginning with the League of Jews and Romans, supposedly in 158 BC, and ending at the downfall of paganism in AD 508—Miller obtaining the date by subtracting 158 from 666. Miller's key statements follow:

> "'And arms shall stand on his part, and they shall pollute the sanctuary of strength, and shall take away the daily sacrifice, and they shall place the abomination that maketh desolate.'
> "By this I understand the same northern nations that should and did conquer the Roman empire, and polluted Rome by the slaughter of her citizens and ravages committed by the armies of the northern barbarians, and after dividing the roman empire into two kingdoms, these two kings being converted to the Christian faith, were the instruments of *taking away the pagan rites and sacrifices*, which Daniel, or the angel denominates the 'daily sacrifice abomination.'
> "Here ends the description of the first beast, in the fourth kingdom, which John informs us in Revelation 13:18 he saw numbered, 'and

his number is six hundred threescore and six,' which I understand to mean the years that this beast, or pagan Rome should contaminate the Jewish and Christian religion, break in pieces and devour with his 'great iron teeth,' the same. If this be a correct exposition of the text, then this beast began his power over the people of God, 158 years before Christ, and would end 508 years after Christ; so that we are brought down to A.D. 508." Miller, "Evidence of Scripture and History of the Second Coming of Christ about the year 1843, and of His personal Reign of 1000 Years." First published in 1833, quoted in *Signs of the Times*, June 15, 1841, p. 41, col. 2, emphasis added.

Miller also involved "666" in his interpretation.

"Then if this be correct, that Pagan Rome began his power in the year B.C. 158, and was to continue 666 years, when would Paganism fall in the Roman kingdom and the 'daily sacrifice abomination,' be taken out of the way to make room for the abomination of desolation? I answer; take 158 from 666 and you will have 508. Then in the year A.D. 508 *Paganism ceased*." Ibid., p. 61 (1838 ed., p. 81), emphasis added.

Miller's view, though, was not widely shared.

"In the evening, Mr. Miller lectured upon the number of the beast in Revelation. He was unusually clear, and seemed to carry conviction to many, of the correctness of his application of this prophecy. He remarked that his Advent brethren had not generally agreed with his views of it, and that satisfied him that they studied the scriptures for themselves, and followed him only so far as they believed he followed the word of God. He was, however, fully satisfied that the number of the beast 666 could only denote the years of pagan Roman supremacy from BC 158 to AD 508." *Midnight Cry*, Feb. 22, 1844, p. 242, col. 3; also in *Advent Herald*, Feb. 14, 1844, p. 9, col. 1.

Even Charles Fitch, Miller's first ministerial convert, questioned the basis of Miller's interpretation of the "daily" in his first letter to Miller.

"March 5, 1838 Will you have the kindness to inform me, by letter, in what history you find the fact stated that the last of the ten kings was baptized in AD 508." Bliss, Sylvester, *Memoirs of William Miller* (Boston, 1853), 129.

Union and consistency before 1844 was enjoyed by those who held the correct view of the supplied word "sacrifice" in relation to the "daily" of Daniel 8, which thus denied any application or connection of the "daily" to Jewish sacrifices. This was a conspicuous and uniform attitude on the part of all Millerites prior to the Disappointment, as these typical declarations witness:

"Jewish Worship Cannot be Intended By the Daily." *Signs of the Times*, May 24, 1843, p. 95, col. 2.
The Daily "Not the Jewish Sacrifice." Ibid., June 21, 1843, p. 126, col. 2.
"Cannot Be the Jewish Sacrifices." Ibid., p. 136, col. 1.

Thus the 1843 chart referred to in *Early Writings*, page seventy-four ("A Chronological Chart of the Visions of Daniel and John"), omitted the AD 33 cross, the 666 years of the pagan Roman beast, and nowhere defined the "daily" as paganism. The chart bore marks of careful revision to eliminate supposition and conjecture, such as had appeared in half a dozen places on the earlier 1841 chart. Doubtful and disputed details were left out, among them the definition of the "daily" as pagan Rome.

On the other hand, the erroneous 158 BC date for the beginning of Roman supremacy was retained, as was the AD 1843 ending of the 2300-year period, the division of Rome in AD 490, etc., which errors obviously constituted the "mistake" in "some of the figures" referred to.

Now that we finally have the historical documentation before us of how one group of Millerites derived their advocated paganism view, let us analyze the facts and assess the platform on which their premise of the "daily" was built.

So far as historical documentation has revealed, we have seen that the so-called "old view" of paganism is really the new view, and the so-called "new view" of Christ's ministry is really the old view. (It sounds confusing, doesn't it? It is, but bear with us.)

If we give to William Miller the date of AD 1831 for the commencement of the paganism view to the present date of 2008, we have a span of 177 years. If we date the commencement of the heavenly sanctuary ministry view in the year AD 1550 to the present, we have a longer span of 458 years. But if we want to be biblical about it, we will begin the heavenly sanctuary ministry view's commencement and understanding via type and antitype in the books of Moses. Now we have thousands of years for what is properly called the "old view." Remember, God's people will call things by their right names.

While William Miller most certainly deserves our respect, the dear brother was not infallible. His identification of the "daily" with paganism was based on his conclusion that it was a term found only in Daniel. He did not compare its usage there with more than one hundred passages in which the original Hebrew word for "daily" is used. In addition, a conclusion based entirely on the use of the verb "take away" in the Greek in a single passage of 2 Thess. 2:7, 8 is decidedly not the designated method to be used for definitive answers, according to the Bible and Spirit of Prophecy. Only by comparing scripture with scripture, "line upon line and precept upon precept," and in context can we safely arrive at valid conclusions.

Brother Miller advocated that the ten-horned beast from the sea (in Rev. 13) was pagan Rome, but we all know that to be false. Ellen White clearly says that the first beast of Revelation 13 is none other than the papacy:

> "The dragon had given to the beast 'his power, and his seat, and great authority.' Revelation 13:2. And now began the 1260 years of papal oppression foretold in the prophecies of Daniel and the Revelation." *Great Controversy*, 54.

Miller also taught that the two-horned beast from the earth in Revelation 13 was the papal image of pa-ganism, the papacy. We know this also to be false, for Ellen White says the two-horned beast is none other than the United States of America:

> "'And he had two horns like a lamb.' The lamblike horns indicate youth, innocence, and gentleness, fitly representing the character of the United States when presented to the prophet as 'coming up' in 1798." Ibid., 441.

Next, Miller preached that the second or papal beast exercised power 1260 years (the forty-two months of verse five), and denoted pagan Rome's period to be 666 years. However, we know that in Revelation 13:18 the "666" is said to be for the number of his name:

> "Here is wisdom. Let him that hath understanding count the number of the beast: for it is the number of a man; and his number is Six hundred threescore and six."

The "666" has nothing to do with years—hence another error: Brother Miller then commenced this time period of 666 years with the League of Jews and Romans, supposedly beginning it in 158 BC, and ending it at the supposed downfall of paganism in AD 508. He obtained the date of 508 by subtracting 158 BC from the 666 (years) of Revelation 13:18. Yet Willie White and history have shown that the League of Jews and Romans was not 158 but 161 BC (Letter to his brother, J. E. White, June 1, 1910, pg. 12). It was only by the hand of God that the 508 date appeared on the 1843 chart at all:

> "I have seen that the 1843 chart was directed by the hand of the Lord, and that it should not be altered; that the figures were as He wanted them." *Early Writings*, 74.

The view that the conversion of pagan kings took away paganism was also disputed. We will now examine that premise. E. J. Hibbard, writing to Elder L. A. Smith (son of Uriah Smith) in San Fernando, CA, on October 24, 1909, addressed this very topic.

> "If we take the inconsistent stand that the Barbarians came to help the Papacy destroy the paganism of Rome, and accomplished this by the destruction of their own paganism, and that this occurred in the year 508, we are doubly mistaken, for not a single one of the Barbaric kingdoms which supplanted the Western Empire of Rome gave up its pagan doctrines and accepted the Papal in the year 508. Clovis, king of the Franks, professed to become a Catholic in the year 496; the Visigoths, now the Spanish, found their first Catholic king in Recared, 586 A.D. Ethelbert, king of Kent, was the first of the Anglo-Saxons to accept the Papal religion, and that was in the year 587. But it was a hundred years later before the whole territory of the Anglo-Saxons accepted the Papal religion. In Germany the Papacy did not get a foothold before the year 687, and it was fully a hundred year later before it, as a nation, had renounced its paganism. You are well aware of the fact that under Charlemagne in the year 772 A.D. began the whole of

thirty-three years for the purpose of Christianizing (?) the Saxons.

"But with the Gospel view of this question, as my article in the SIGNS briefly opens it, everything is in harmony, even to the matter of dates. In fact, the very argument in Daniel and the Revelation, used to establish the fall of Paganism in 508, rather teaches the contrary; and shows that a general war against heresy began in the Eastern Empire in the year 508 and continued ten years.

"The quotation in part reads as follows:- 'Three furious, but transient seditions, were encouraged by the success of Vitalian, who, with an army of Huns and Bulgarians for the most part idolaters, declared himself the champion of the Catholic faith. In this pious rebellion he depopulated Thrace, besieged Constantinople, exterminated 65,000 of his fellow Christians, till he obtained the recall of the bishops, the satisfaction of the pope, and the establishment of the council of Calcedon, an orthodox treaty, reluctantly signed by the dying Anastasius, and more faithfully performed by the uncle of Justinian. And such was the event of the first of the religious wars which have been waged in the name, and by the disciples, of the God of Peace.'"

How can a war waged by the disciples of the God of Peace against their fellow Christians, beginning in the year AD 508 and continuing ten years or until 65,000 of their fellow Christians were exterminated, have anything to do with the taking away of paganism? To this day there has been no response to this inquiry. Why? Simply put, because there is no historical foundation whatsoever for the premise advocated by William Miller. Thus we come to the hard fact that William Miller's only correct position on the "daily" was his adherence to the correct date of AD 508—and that was only by the hand of God.

Let us now turn our attention to those who, before 1844, were advocating the ministerial work of Christ as the "daily." What was their understanding and application of the term? It was that the "daily" is the continual mediation of Christ in the heavenly sanctuary:

> "The very heart of the gospel was removed when the little horn took away the daily or continual mediation of Jesus Christ, and cast down the place of his gospel sanctuary and made it a den of thieves. He cast down the sacraments and gospel truth to the ground and 'practiced' the mystery of iniquity and prospered in his sacrilegious perversions. The little horn and his part of the host had indignation against the covenant; that is, the blood of the covenant, by trampling virtually upon the son of God, and counting the blood of the covenant an unholy thing. They cast down the true doctrine of the cross of Christ, the crucified One. They cast down the table of the gospel show bread, which was both a 'munition of rocks' and a 'sanctuary of strength' to the church. The great matter to be taken away was the righteousness of Christ. The unbelieving Jews set the example. Away with this man and his righteousness and give us Barabbas, the robber, and his righteousness. Away with Jesus Christ and give us the Pope, the usurper of Christ's throne. The great doctrine of Antichrist is, the Pope is the corrector of heretics. This was established AD 538. Then where two or three poor souls were assembled together in Christ's name, in times of peril, there he would be a little sanctuary for them there am I in the midst of them. Then the papal armies would persecute them, and cast down the place of Christ's sanctuary. Dan.8:11, decides whose sanctuary it was. It is His sanctuary. Only two personages have been introduced to whom the word his can possibly apply. One was the Pope,

the other was Jesus Christ, the Prince. None will say it was the Pope's the man of sin. Therefore it was the sanctuary of the Lord Jesus Christ. Now take two passages perfectly parallel. One is, his sanctuary was cast down; the other is, the truth [was] cast down. Who can doubt the identity. The Word the Truth, was made flesh and dwelt among us, and that flesh was 'sacrificed for us' and that 'sacrifice' was 'taken away' and that 'truth' was 'cast down to the ground." *Midnight Cry*, Oct. 4, 1843, p. 52, cols 2, 3. (The White Estate believes the author was O. R. L. Crosier.)

Thus far we have accurately disclosed both sides' positions on the "daily" prior to 1844 in their own words. We now will focus on their united understanding of the "daily" after the Disappointment of 1844.

Crosier's presentation on the sanctuary was built upon the biblical principle of type preceding and illustrating anti-type, with the basic premise being that the sanctuary of Dan. 8:11–14 to be cleansed in 1844 was the heavenly sanctuary, connected with the New Jerusalem and involving Christ's two-fold ministry therein. After stressing that the sanctuary was the heart of the typical system, Crosier showed that the old covenant is connected with the earthly sanctuary and the new covenant with the heavenly sanctuary, into which our High Priest entered to minister. Essential paragraphs of his argument, based on the interpretation of the "daily" as Christ's mediation, follow:

> "The Sanctuary to be cleansed at the end of the 2300 days is also the Sanctuary of the new covenant, for the vision of the treading down and cleansing, is after the crucifixion. We see that the Sanctuary of the new covenant is not on earth, but in heaven." Crosier, *The Day-Star (Extra)*, Feb. 7, 1846, p. 38, col. 1.
> 
> "The Sanctuary of the new covenant is connected with New Jerusalem, like the Sanctuary of the

first covenant was with Old Jerusalem. As that was the place where the priests of that covenant ministered, so this is in heaven, the place where the Priest of the new covenant ministers. To these places, and these only, the N. T. applies the name 'Sanctuary,' and it does appear that this should forever set the question at rest.

"But as we have been so long and industriously taught to look to the earth for the Sanctuary, it may be proper to inquire, by what scriptural authority have we been thus taught? I can find none. If others can, let them produce it." Ibid., p. 38, col. 2.

"Introduced by this question, 'Is the earth, is Palestine such a place?' The entire contents answer, No! Was Daniel so taught? Look at his vision." Ibid.

Crosier continues:

"'And the place of his Sanctuary was cast down;' Dan. 8:11. This casting down was in the days and by means of the Roman power; therefore, the Sanctuary of this text was not the Earth, nor Palestine, because the former was cast down at the fall, more than 4000 years, and the latter at the captivity, more than 700 years previous to the event of this passage, and neither by Roman agency.

"The Sanctuary cast down is his against whom Roman magnified himself, which was the Prince of the host, Jesus Christ; and Paul teaches that his Sanctuary is in heaven. Again, Dan. 11:30, 31, 'For the ships of Chittim shall have come against him; therefore shall he be grieved and return, and have indignation (the staff to chastise) against the holy covenant (Christianity), so shall he do; he shall even return and have intelligence with them (priests and bishops); that forsake the holy covenant. And arms (civil and religious) shall stand on his part, and they (Rome and those that forsake the holy covenant) shall pollute the Sanctuary of strength.' What was this that Rome and the [apostate] apostles of Christianity should jointly pollute? This combination was formed against the 'holy covenant' and it was the Sanctuary of that covenant they polluted; which they could do as well as to pollute the name of God; Jer. 34:16; Ezek. 20; Mal. 1:7. This was the same as profaning or blaspheming his name. In this sense this 'politico-religious' beast polluted the Sanctuary, (Rev. 13:6) and cast it down from its place in heaven, (Ps. 102-19; Jer. 17:12; Heb 8:1, 2) when they called Rome the holy city (Rev. 21:2) and enstalled [*sic*] the Pope there with the titles, 'Lord God the Pope,' 'Holy Father,' 'Head of the Church,' etc., and there in the counterfeit 'temple of God' he professes to do what Jesus actually does in his Sanctuary; 2 Thess. 2:1-8. The Sanctuary has been trodden underfoot (Dan. 8:13), the same as the Son of God has. Heb. 10:29." Ibid., p. 38, col. 2.

In 1846, Joseph Bates commended the Crosier article as "superior:"

> "But allow me first to recommend to your particular notice, O. R. L. Crosier's article in the Day-Star Extra, for the 7th of February, 1846, from the 37th to the 44th page. Read it again. In my humble opinion it is superior to anything of the kind extant." Bates, *The Opening Heavens*, May 8, 1846, p. 25.

One year later, Ellen White commended the same article to everyone:

> "The Lord shew me in vision, more than one year ago, that Brother Crosier had the true light, on the cleansing of the Sanctuary, etc.; and that it

was His will, that Brother Crosier should write out the view which he gave us in the Day-Star Extra, February 7, 1846. I feel fully authorized by the Lord, to recommend that Extra, to every saint." White, E. G., *A Word to the Little Flock*, May 1846, p. 12.

David Arnold, a frequent contributor to *Present Truth* and one of publishing committee of five for *Advent Review*, published the following, affirming the end of the "daily" mediation in 1844:

"Therefore, we are brought, by the force of circumstances, and the fulfillment of events, to the irresistible conclusion that, on the tenth day of the seventh month, (Jewish time), in the autumn of 1844, Christ did close his daily, or continual ministration or mediation in the first apartment of the heavenly sanctuary, and shut the door, which no man can open; and opened a door, in the second apartment, or Holiest of all, which no man can shut, (see Rev. 3: 7- 8), and passed within the second vail, bearing before the Father, on the breast-plate of judgment, all for whom He is now acting as intercessor." *Present Truth*, Dec. 1849, p. 45, col. 2.

Four months after James White reprinted Crosier's article in full in the regular *Advent Review* of September 1850, and omitted sections of the article from a forty-eight-page special *Review* for wider circulation among non-Sabbatarian Adventists of the former movement, he paralleled Crosier's view when he wrote:

"Those that teach that 'the promised land' is the Sanctuary must, therefore, admit that the words 'trodden under foot,' and 'trodden down,' are figurative expressions, and mean that the promised land has been overrun with 'the wicked agents of its desolation.' Then they should not object to our using the expressions figuratively, in applying the words 'trodden down' (Isa. 63:18) to the typical Sanctuary, and the words 'trodden under foot' (Dan. 8:13) to 'the true Tabernacle' or 'Sanctuary' in heaven.

"It may be said that the heavenly Sanctuary is not 'capable of being trodden under foot.' But we ask, is it not as capable of being trodden under foot as the Son of God,' who is the 'MINISTER' of the same Sanctuary? Says Paul: "Of how much sorer punishment, suppose ye, shall he be thought worthy, who hath TRODDEN UNDER FOOT THE SON OF GOD, and hath counted the blood of the covenant, wherewith he was sanctified, an unholy thing, and hath done despite unto the Spirit of Grace.' Heb. 10:29.

"We say, then, the Sanctuary in heaven has been trodden under foot in the same sense that the Son of God has been trodden underfoot. In a similar manner has the 'host,' the true church, also, been trodden down. Those who have rejected the Son of God have trodden him under foot, and of course have trodden under foot His Sanctuary.

"The Catholic Church have trodden under foot, not only the 'Holy City,' but the Sanctuary, and its Minister, or Priest, 'the Son of God.' Rome has been called 'the Holy City,' and the 'Eternal City,' which can only be said of the City of the living God; the New Jerusalem.

"The Pope has professed to have 'power on earth to forgive sins,' which power belongs alone to Christ. The people have been taught to look to 'the man of sin,' seated in his temple, or as Paul says—'so that he as God sitteth in the temple of God,' etc.—instead of looking to Jesus, seated at the right hand of the Father, in the heavenly Sanctuary. In thus turning away from Jesus, who alone could forgive sins, and give eternal life, and in bestowing on the Pope such titles as MOST HOLY LORD, they have 'trodden underfoot the

Son of God.' And in calling Rome the 'Eternal City,' and the 'Holy City,' they have trodden down the City of the living God, and the heavenly Sanctuary. The 'host,' the true church that have looked to Jesus in the true Sanctuary for pardon of sins, and eternal life, has, as well as their Divine Lord and His Sanctuary, been trodden under foot. Yes, the true worshipers have been rejected and persecuted, and some of the brightest 'stars,' or gospel ministers, in the church have been 'stamped upon' by the little horn." *Review and Herald*, Jan. 1851, pp. 28, 29.

Uriah Smith also confirmed Crosier's interpretation.

"Again, we read in Dan. 8:13, about treading the Sanctuary under foot; and it may be asked how a Sanctuary in heaven can be trodden under foot. These expressions are figurative as will be seen by Hebrews 10:29, which speaks of treading underfoot the Son of God. The Sanctuary can be trodden underfoot in the same sense that the Son of God, its minister can. Thus the Pope has trodden underfoot the Sanctuary, by calling his own sanctuary, or temple, the temple of God, and turning away the worship of men from the temple of God in heaven to his own sanctuary at Rome. And he has trodden underfoot the Son of God, the minister of that Sanctuary, by exalting himself above all that is called God, and assuming to be the head of the church in the place of Jesus Christ." *Review and Herald*, March 28, 1854.

Thus from these excerpts it can be seen that after 1844, when the earth was not "cleansed," another sanctuary had to be considered, as well as another "daily," even by staunch paganism proponents. He whose sanctuary is being cleansed is the same "He" whose "daily" intercession there was usurped or "taken away" by the papal beast.

# 3

## EXPOSITION OF *EARLY WRITINGS*, 74–76

Before going any further in our history, we need to return to the year 1850 and ask for what reason Ellen White penned those well-known controversial words in *Early Writings*, 74–76. Much of the current confusion about the "daily" is caused by words being supplied to that passage. We begin by separating the myths from the facts.

At the turn of the century, W. W. Prescott, confronting the same issue of the conflicting meanings of the "daily," stood on a platform that should be agreeable to all:

> "Every interpretation of a fulfilled prophecy must be in harmony with facts; and questions of difference are to be settled, not by mere assertions or unwarranted claims, but by such evidence as will stand the closest examination. It should be our sincere aim to know and teach the truth, and we should be prepared to do what we are constantly asking others to do, viz., to accept evidence, and to change our views when they are proved to be incorrect. It is no discredit to a sincere man to be found mistaken, but he discredits himself when he refuses to correct a mistake which has been plainly pointed out. It is more important to know the truth than to cling to a traditional teaching." *The Daily*, p. 1 (pamphlet).

By the grace of God, we endeavor to stand on that same platform. Thus far in review, we have documented that the Bible supports only one definition of the "daily"—that of the "continual" ministry of the priest in the holy place. Nowhere does the Bible endorse the view that the "daily" is paganism. We documented how Ellen White was at odds with nearly every point of William Miller's theology surrounding the "daily." In distinct contrast, she fully endorsed Brother Crosier's position and commended it to every saint as a result of a vision in which the Lord showed her that Crosier had the "true light, on the cleansing of the Sanctuary" and that "it was His will, that Brother Crosier should write out that view." (White, E. G., *A Word to the Little Flock*, May 1846, p. 12.) Crosier's position was the ministry of Christ, and the "sanctuary" being none other than the sanctuary of Christ. In addition, we saw that James White's and Uriah Smith's writings paralleled Brother Crosier's.

With those facts now before us, how can any searcher for truth maintain a belief that Ellen White was endorsing William Miller's view of the "daily" being paganism in her account of her vision of September 23, 1850, recorded in *Early Writings*, 74–76? Yet controversy and division have persisted in our ranks on that very topic, so it is appropriate now to address the issue from a different perspective.

The *Early Writings* passage in question is here provided for easy reference, beginning with the last sentence of the first paragraph:

> "I have seen that the 1843 chart was directed by the hand of the Lord, and that it should not be altered; that the figures were as He wanted them; that His hand was over and hid a mistake in some of the figures, so that none could see it, until His hand was removed.
> 
> "Then I saw in relation to the 'daily' (Daniel 8:12) that the word 'sacrifice' was supplied by man's wisdom, and does not belong to the text, and that the Lord gave the correct view of it to those who gave the judgment hour cry. When union existed, before 1844, nearly all were united on the correct view of the 'daily'; but in the confusion since 1844, other views have been embraced, and darkness and confusion have followed. Time has not been a test since 1844, and it will never again be a test.
> 
> "The Lord has shown me that the message of the third angel must go, and be proclaimed to the

scattered children of the Lord, but it must not be hung on time. I saw that some were getting a false excitement, arising from preaching time; but the third angel's message is stronger than time can be. I saw that this message can stand on its own foundation and needs not time to strengthen it; and that it will go in mighty power, and do its work, and will be cut short in righteousness.

"Then I was pointed to some who are in the great error of believing that it is their duty to go to Old Jerusalem, and think they have a work to do there before the Lord comes. Such a view is calculated to take the mind and interest from the present work of the Lord, under the message of the third angel; for those who think that they are yet to go to Jerusalem will have their minds there, and their means will be withheld from the cause of present truth to get themselves and others there. I saw that such a mission would accomplish no real good, that it would take a long while to make a very few of the Jews believe even in the first advent of Christ, much more to believe in His second advent. I saw that Satan had greatly deceived some in this thing and that souls all around them in this land could be helped by them and led to keep the commandments of God, but they were leaving them to perish. I also saw that Old Jerusalem never would be built up; and that Satan was doing his utmost to lead the minds of the children of the Lord into these things now, in the gathering time, to keep them from throwing their whole interest into the present work of the Lord, and to cause them to neglect the necessary preparation for the day of the Lord." *Early Writings*, 74–76.

Before we begin to fully dissect this quotation and show its true meaning and implications from the words of Ellen White herself, we must review the cautionary counsel she has given to all of us regarding the use of this *Early Writings* passage as a so-called proof text to establish that Ellen White supported the position that the "daily" is paganism. The following documentation will reveal that nothing could be further from the truth.

> "I have words to speak to my brethren east and west, north and south. I request that my writings shall not be used as the leading argument to settle questions over which there is now so much controversy. I intreat [*sic*] of Elders H, I, J, [Haskell, Loughborough, Smith] and others of our leading brethren that they make no reference to my writings to sustain their views of 'the daily.' I now ask that my ministering brethren shall not make use of my writings in their arguments regarding this question; for I have had no instruction on the point under discussion." *Selected Messages*, 1:164.

In the original letter of July 31, 1910, found in *Manuscript 11*, 1910, she directly targeted and named Haskell, Loughborough and Smith, who were promoting the paganism view, and others who pointed to her writings, claiming those sentences in *Early Writings* were upholding their mistaken supposition of the "daily." Ellen White forthrightly checked this misuse of her writings by demanding that they should *not* be used to settle the different views of the "daily." Yet today, how many still use *Early Writings*, 74–76, for this very argument, wholly disregarding the plain counsel of the Lord! The reason was stated in that letter so that none need err:

> "I have had no instruction on the point under discussion."

Thus in Ellen White's own words, we read she had received no light on the "daily." And she affirmed that once again during an interview with A. G. Daniells, accompanied by Willie C. White and C. C. Crisler, wherein she could not be drawn out to speak on a topic on which she had "no instruction."

What follows is an account of Elder A. G. Daniells regarding that interview he had with Ellen White. Elder Daniells was trying to learn her position on the "daily." The account is entitled "A Statement by Elder A. G. Daniells regarding an Interview with Mrs. E. G. White relative to the 'Daily' of Daniel."

> "When we were having some controversy regarding what we called the 'daily' of Dan. 8:9-14, those who argued for the old view [paganism] claimed that it was supported by the following statement on page 74 of 'Early Writings':
>
> "'Then I saw in relation to the 'daily,' Dan. 8:12, that the word 'sacrifice' was supplied by man's wisdom, and does not belong to the text; and that the Lord gave the correct view of it to those who gave the judgment-hour cry. When union existed, before 1844, nearly all were united on the correct view of the 'daily;' but in the confusion since 1844, other views have been embraced, and darkness and confusion have followed. Time has not been a test since 1844, and it will never again be a test.'
>
> "I first read to Sister White the statement given above, in 'Early Writings.' Then I placed before her our prophetic chart used by our ministers in expounding the prophecies of Daniel and Revelation. I called her attention to the picture of the Sanctuary and also to the 2300 year period as they appeared on the chart.
>
> "I then asked if she could recall what was shown her regarding this subject.
>
> "As I recall her answer she began by telling how some of the leaders who had been in the 1844 movement endeavored to find new dates for the termination of the 2300 year period. This endeavor was to fix new dates for the coming of the Lord. This was causing confusion among

those who had been in the Advent movement.

"In this confusion the Lord revealed to her, she said, that the view that had been held and presented regarding the dates was correct, and that there must never be another time set, nor another time message.

"I then asked her to tell what had been revealed to her about the rest of the 'daily,' the Prince, the host, the taking away of the 'daily' and the casting down of the sanctuary.

"She replied that these features were not placed before her in vision as the time part was. She would not be led out to make an explanation of those points of the prophecy.

"The interview made a deep impression on my mind. Without hesitation she talked freely, clearly, and at length about the 2300 year period, but regarding the other part of the prophecy she was silent.

"The only conclusion I could draw from her free explanation of the time and her silence as to the taking away of the 'daily' and the casting down of the sanctuary was that the vision given her was regarding the time, and that she receive no explanation as to the other parts of the prophecy."

Amazing as it may seem, given her prophetic gift, Ellen White could give no explanation of the "daily" beyond the context of correct and incorrect dates. No wonder, then, her demand not to use her writings to settle the differences on the definition of the "daily." This demand she even personally conveyed to Elder Haskell in a letter dated August 28, 1908, with a rebuke for using the 1843 chart, as he had been claiming that the chart and *Early Writings*, 74–75, endorsed the view of paganism. Regarding this, Ellen White wrote:

> "To you also I say that this subject should not be agitated at this time. Now, my brother, I feel

that at this crisis in our experience that chart which you have had republished should not be circulated. You have made a mistake in this matter. Elder Haskell, I am unable to define clearly the points that are questioned."

In that letter to Haskell she again affirmed that she had received no light on the "daily." Nowhere on the 1843 chart or in the writings of Ellen White is there a connection or a statement that the "daily" is paganism that was "taken away" or removed in AD 508 or 538.

It should now be clear to all why God gave His instruction to Ellen White to call the brethren to come together and study out the issue of the "daily." That instruction to study necessarily included investigation of the ministry-of-Christ view of Brother Daniells and others who were advocating that position. All were charged to come into unity as soon as possible, as quoted from Letter 50, 1910, to the Haskells (*Manuscript Releases*, Vol. 20, 223). In that letter she placed the burden of proof and the initiation of investigation of differing viewpoints *not* on those holding the ministry-of-Christ view, but on the adherents of the paganism view. Her demand was that Haskell and "others of our ministering brethren in this conference" meet with Elder Daniells, "listen to his reasons," and either sustain their own position with documentation and facts or concede to his documentation and facts. Her saying "Our brethren should listen to his [Daniells'] reasons, and give candid consideration to his views" is clear evidence that Ellen White did not believe Daniells was advocating spiritualistic concepts, as is sometimes alleged today. Had he been guilty of doing so, she then would have been advocating consideration of such heresy. This point will be addressed more fully at the appropriate time.

Yet as insurmountable a dilemma as this long-standing "daily" controversy may appear to be, there is a logical, totally defensible and rather simple resolution, as all will see in the upcoming paragraphs. Unity on this topic need no longer be delayed.

We begin with some background. Mrs. White's oft-quoted allusion to the "daily" in *Early Writings* appeared in *Present Truth* of November 1850 (p. 87), her written account having resulted from a vision received on September 23, 1850. Those paragraphs were then placed in the initial *Experience and Views*, published in August 1851 (pp. 61, 62).

Her references were unmistakably to contemporary agitations and deflections, chiefly among First-day Adventists, who had rejected advanced sanctuary and Sabbath light, Spirit of Prophecy guidance, and the integrity of the 2300-year dates, and who were setting terminal dates forward from year to year. Immediately after the Disappointment in 1844, time-setting had begun, arising from disputes among chronologists about a few years, and particularly regarding different dates projected for the cross. Time-setting involved new times for each of the three key dates—the beginning year, the crucifixion year, and the end year. These aberrant positions were affecting even some Sabbatarian Adventists, hence the counsel in *Early Writings*.

Three distinct but related items were emphasized in successive and contingent "time-a-test" statements within the four paragraphs. These three consecutive points were: (1) commendation of Fitch's 1843 chart, with God's hand hiding a mistake in some of the figures; (2) the "daily," the word "sacrifice" supplied, and time being a test; and (3) agitation by some that the saints were yet to go to Old Jerusalem.

The first in her series of points came in the paragraph pertaining to the 1843 chart:

> "The Lord showed me that the 1843 chart was directed by His hand, and that no part of it should be altered; that the figures were as He wanted them. That His hand was over and hid a mistake in some of the figures, so that none could see it, until His hand was removed." White, E. G., *Present Truth*, Nov. 1850, p. 87, col. 1. (Reprinted in *Experience and Views*, 1851, p. 61.)

The constant time-setting which characterized certain nominal Adventists involved denial of the verity of the former movement and the validity of its time argument. James White therefore wrote:

> "Since the 2300 days ended in 1844, quite a number of times have been set, by different individuals for their termination. In doing this they have removed the 'landmarks' and have thrown darkness and doubt over the whole advent movement." (White, James, Note 2, *Present Truth*, May 1850, p. 74, col. 2.)

Why did some even begin to set new dates for Christ's Second Advent? It was because of their failure to accept their mistake in their definition of the "sanctuary." After the Great Disappointment, when Christ had not come as expected to cleanse the earth, a determined examination of the scriptures (*Great Controversy*, 411) brought the more accurate understanding that the sanctuary in Daniel 8:14 was the *heavenly* sanctuary, and that Jesus had just entered the second apartment to begin the antitypical Day of Atonement. Fortunately, some accepted the light of instruction. With that unmistakable light, the searching, faithful ones in the Advent movement, if they had not already done so, accepted the glorious ministry-of-Christ view. (See *Spiritual Gifts*, Vol. 1, 148–50.) Unfortunately, others rejected that same light on the sanctuary.

It is no wonder Ellen White was distressed by the divisions and distractions that manifested soon after this sanctuary and ministry-of-Christ light was revealed. Instead of proclaiming the third angel's message, much time and energy was expended by both sides in propounding or protesting against different unsustainable times of Christ's near return or new "other views" that would derail or delay the progress of the movement.

Then about 1849, a new argument was introduced and a new basis for the 2300-year calculation was projected by nominal Adventists. They revived the supplied word "sacrifice" in relation to the "daily," contending that this

Biblical pairing of words meant Jewish sacrifices and setting new times on this new basis.

One writer stated his ideas thus:

> "In the phrase 'daily sacrifice' (Dan. 8:11, 12), the word 'sacrifice' is italicized to indicate that it is supplied by the translator. The qualifying term must be understood as included within itself, so that the word 'sacrifice' is correctly supplied. It is then the continual Jewish sacrificial observances, which were terminated by Rome, symbolized by the little horn, at the destruction of Jerusalem. In other words, how long will be the fulfilling of the vision in which is presented the termination of the Jewish service and the transgression of Rome, to accomplish the trampling down of the Sanctuary and the holy people?" Ed., *Advent Herald*, Mar. 3, 1849, p. 36, cols. 2, 3.
>
> "'The Place of his sanctuary.' It must, consequently, we think, have reference to the desolation of the temple which was cast down by the Romans, when they took away the continual burnt offerings. The casting down the truth to the ground—of its persecuting Christianity, as well as destroying the Jewish worship." Ibid., col. 3.

Some were convinced Jewish sacrifices were meant.

> "Mr. Miller, perceiving the prophecy referred to the government of Rome, the fourth kingdom, supposed 'the daily sacrifice' to be paganism, and A.D. 508, to be the point where it was 'taken away;' and believing 'the abomination of desolation' to be papacy, he deemed the decree of Justinian to be the point where it was 'set up.' But we are led to differ from Mr. Miller in regard to the meaning of the 'daily,' and from other writers referred to, in regard to its application.

> That the Jewish sacrifices are alluded to by the term 'daily,' there can be no doubt. The term is borrowed from the sacerdotal offerings of the Jewish worship." Berwick, F. H., *The Lord Soon to Come* (Boston, 1854), p. 82.

A picture of a Jewish sacrificial altar was included on a chart by Cummings in 1854. The chart showed a revised beginning of the 2300-year period, now made to begin in 446 BC, and terminating 2300 years later in AD 1854—thus setting time and making that time a test, on the basis of inserting "sacrifice" into the text.

> "The Jewish altar is to represent the daily sacrifices of God's people from the time the covenant was entered into, which restored their worship." Cummings, J., *Explanation of the Prophetic Chart* (Concord, 1854), p. 3.
> "It will clearly be seen where 'the daily sacrifice' (true worship) commenced, consequently where the 2300 days (years) commence of Dan. 8:14 The daily sacrifice commencing with the 2300 days (years), about 446 B.C." Ibid., p. 7.
> "Will future events come in their time? Yes. THEN THE LORD WILL COME THIS YEAR, 1854." Ibid., p. 246. (Cummings' articles were running through the *Advent Herald* in 1849, when the first "Jewish sacrifices" assumptions appeared.)

Even Joseph Bates was affected by the time-setting emphasis of the period. Although holding tenaciously to the integrity of the 457 BC beginning and AD 1844 terminal dates, he temporarily held the idea that the duration of Christ's ministry in the Most Holy Place would be seven years—from 1844 to 1851. This he published in 1850 in *Explanation of the Typical and Anti-typical Sanctuary*.

Loughborough identified in print the originators of the discord.

> "The 'confusion' that came in after the termination of the 2300 days was first among those who persisted in setting times for the Lord to come. They claimed that the 'daily sacrifice' meant the Jewish daily offerings. That certainly made 'confusion' in what were the clear views before." (Loughborough, J. N., *Review and Herald*, April 4, 1907, p. 10, col. 1.)

Thus the basis of the "confusion" mentioned by Mrs. White was publicly recognized and the reason for her reproof made obvious. Thus also the Jewish sacrifice perspective, and the confusion from time-setting resulting from it, was the focus of her second point in the record of her vision in *Early Writings*, 74–76:

> "Then I saw in relation to the 'daily,' that the word 'sacrifice' was supplied by man's wisdom, and does not belong to the text; and that the Lord gave the correct view of it to those who gave the judgment hour cry. When union existed before 1844, nearly all were united on the correct view of the 'daily;' but since 1844, in the confusion, other views have been embraced, and darkness and confusion has followed.
> "The Lord showed me that time had not been a test since 1844, and that time will never again be a test." (In all subsequent printings, this last sentence is run in as a concluding sentence of the paragraph.) White, E. G., *Present Truth*, Nov. 1850, p. 87, col. 1.

Mrs. White's third point was made in paragraph four of the *Early Writings* passage under investigation. It pertained to the agitation beginning in 1849 regarding the final return of Jews to Old Jerusalem in 1850, which interpretation was likewise seeking entrance among our pioneers.

One of the chief contrasts between Old World and New World Advent awakenings was the freedom in

America from the "return-of-the-Jews" fallacy courted by overseas Adventists. The '43 and Seventh Month movements in America were both free from its blight. But after the Disappointment, in an extremist sector, a Jerusalem enterprise was projected which was fostered by a Mrs. C. S. Minor and involved a man in Jerusalem named Messullam.

Hiram Edson temporarily espoused the general back-to-Jerusalem idea, writing an eight-page tract in 1850 on that viewpoint. His published words, in part:

> "That there is to be a literal gathering, or return, of the Jews to the literal land of Israel, the land of Palestine, before the coming of the Lord, is most clearly taught in the Old and the New Testament. The Jews are to be in the land of their fathers, the land of Israel, and in Jerusalem in the time of the battle of the great day of God Almighty." Edson, *Exposition of Scripture Prophecy; Showing the Final Return of the Jews in 1850* (Canandaigua, NY, 1849), p. 3.

In the third of the related statements by Ellen White, she plainly reproved those who advocated that view:

> "Then I was pointed to some who are in the great error, that the saints are yet to go to Old Jerusalem, etc., before the Lord comes. Such a view is calculated to take the mind and interest from the present work of God, under the message of the third angel; for if we are to go to Jerusalem, then our minds will naturally be there, and our means will be withheld from other uses, to get the saints to Jerusalem." White, E. G., *Present Truth*, November 1850, p. 87, col. 1.

As history certainly reveals, the period from 1844 to 1850 was one of marked confusion among Advent believers who passed through the Great Disappointment. Time-setting by nominal Adventists beset the little Sabbatarian group on one hand, with extremists on the other. They struggled against this dual pressure. Such conditions were the background and setting for the subsequent notable vision of September 23, 1850, recorded in *Early Writings*. Obviously, then, on the individual and collective bases of those four related paragraphs, Mrs. White was meeting contemporary developments in time-setting and saints-to-Jerusalem agitations. Over and over again, the central issue, without question, was the issue of time and the setting of new dates—hence the need for the counsel. The overriding concern of the post-1844 movement was the damaging efforts of some to change the historical dates related to the 2300-year prophecy. The paramount issue to be defended was the true dating of the great 2300-year period.

During the same year and in the very month that Mrs. White's "daily" and making-time-a-test paragraph appeared in *Present Truth* (Nov. 1850), the first number of the *Second Advent Review and Sabbath Herald* appeared. In that inaugural issue, Bates wrote thus concerning the question of the prophetic 2300-year "time" and time–setting:

> "For six successive years, viz: from the fall of 1844 to the spring and fall of 1850, the most of these leading members have been aiding and assisting each other in changing the chronology, i.e. the world's history; to prove that they were on the true position. What have they gained? Answer, nothing but disappointment and confusion. This, too, in direct opposition to their standard work. (Advent Shield.) It has not proved to be their shield, that is clear. Six times, did we say! Yes, more. Some have moved the time for the termination of the 2300 days, from fall to spring, for six years in succession, and thus they have almost finished a circle, (if seven years would make one) instead of gaining one inch the right way." Bates, *Review and Herald*, Nov. 1850, p.7, col. 2.

One month later, in December 1850, James White wrote in the *Review and Herald* concerning the integrity of the 2300 days as from 457 BC to AD 1844, particularly on the immovable character of the 457 date (which was now constantly shifted forward by time-setting Adventists), and on the relationship of this basic date to the 1843 chart, asserting:

> "The 2300 Days. This prophetic period has been, and still is, the main pillar of the Advent faith. It is, therefore of the utmost importance that we have a correct view of the commencement and termination of this period, in order to understand our present position." White, J., *Review and Herald*, Dec. 1850, p. 13, col. 1.
>
> "It was the *united* testimony of Second Advent lecturers and papers, when standing on 'the original faith,' that the publication of the chart was a fulfillment of Hab. 2:2, 3. If the chart was a subject of prophecy, (and those who deny it leave the original faith), then it follows that B.C. 457 was the year from which to date the 2300 days. It was necessary that 1843 should be the first published time in order that 'the vision' should 'tarry,' or that there should be a tarrying time, in which the virgin band was to slumber and sleep on the great subject of time, just before they were to be aroused by the Midnight Cry." Ibid., emphasis added.

It was in the midst of such strong statements and earnest contending for the integrity of the established 2300-year dates and denying of all subsequent time-setting proclivities that Ellen White enunciated and reenunciated fundamental principles regarding time-setting and the complete separation of the third angel's message from any time-setting test. These words are from the third paragraph of the *Early Writings* passage:

> "The Lord has shown me that the message of the third angel must go, and be proclaimed to

the scattered children of the Lord, and that it should not be hung on time; for time never will be a test again. I saw that some were getting a false excitement arising from preaching time; that the third angel's message was stronger that time can be. I saw that this message can stand on its own foundation, and that it needs not time to strengthen it, and that it will go in mighty power, and do its work, and will be cut short in righteousness." Vision of June 21, 1851, *Record Book I*, pp. 102, 167; published in *Review and Herald Extra*, July 21, 1851, p. 4, col. 2; and then permanently in *Experience and Views* (original ed. of Aug. 1851).

We now move to a grammatical study of the *Early Writings* passage under discussion, and particularly of the second paragraph around which confusion about the "daily" seems to center.

The first paragraph ends with a reference to calculation mistakes regarding dates involved with the 2300-year prophecy of Daniel 8:14—mistakes that had been corrected by the time of her writing.

In the second paragraph, Ellen White proceeds to state the first of two matters upon which the pioneers agreed, for the most part, prior to 1844. That paragraph begins with a reference to "sacrifice" in relation to the "daily" of Daniel 8. She states that those who gave the judgment hour cry had a "correct view" in their understanding that "sacrifice" was a supplied word. Note that she neither focused on nor defended the "daily" in this statement; her point was limited to the supplied word "sacrifice."

The second sentence in the second paragraph is a compound sentence, meaning it has two main clauses or sentences—divided in this case by a semicolon. The first half of the compound sentence begins with an introductory clause related to time: "when union existed, before 1844." Unity is linked to a time period. Then the main clause tells us what the source or nature of that unity was when "union existed, before 1844." We learn that in that specified time period, "nearly all were united on the *correct view* of the 'daily.'" This "correct view" is the second area of consensus or near-consensus before 1844. Thus two "correct views" were held by those who gave the judgment hour cry: of the supplied word "sacrifice" and of the "daily."

The only information directly provided concerning the "correct view of the 'daily'" in this passage is that there was a near-unanimous view of it before 1844. The historical and grammatical context of the sentence does not suggest that the correctness was in the definition or interpretation of the term. Rather, the entire context points toward correctness on the basis of time or dating. We also know that even scholars opposing the advent movement could find no flaw with the pioneer reckoning for the termination of the 2300-year prophecy. On that matter, therefore, there was unity. Within the advent movement, confidence in the "figures" gave power to proclaim the first and second angels' message.

In a manner parallel to the first half of the compound sentence, the second half of the compound sentence also begins with an introductory phrase that also links a situation or condition with a time period. However, although in parallel construction, the content is contrasting. The situation described is not unity but "confusion," and the time period: "*since* 1844." The main clause again tells us what the circumstances were during the specified time period, i.e., the source of the confusion. In stark contrast to the unity of the first half of the compound sentence, we learn in the second half that confusion had been brought about because "*other views* have been embraced."

Immediately after her identification of the problem being "other views being embraced," we rightly anticipate that details to substantiate the statement of fact she just made will now follow. We begin to read what those confusing "other views" were. In the third and final sentence of the second paragraph, we learn that the primary matter of concern expressed by Ellen White as a result of her vision is that "time is not to be a test" after 1844. In other words, new dates were not to be set for Christ's return. The writer's concern was that the departure from reasoned *unity* based on the unassailable date was leading to growing *disunity* due to new time-setting. Instead of bringing new light, the "other views" for the termination of the 2300-year prophecy were causing considerable "darkness and confusion."

In the compound sentence, the "*correct view* of the 'daily'" is plainly contrasted with the "other views," which we know are *incorrect views*. The term "other views"—to be distinguished from "the correct view"—can mean only "incorrect" views. Both correct and incorrect views are in the context of the "daily" of Daniel 8:13 regarding time fulfillment. Neither one has anything to do with the *definition* of the "daily." Both views refer only to the contemporary fulfillment of the 2300-year prophecy. The anticipated event was their consuming focus. The "time" was at hand.

The unity of the first half of the compound sentence was based on shared confidence in the unchallenged date of termination of that prophecy: 1844. Those calculations "were directed by the hand of the Lord." It wasn't until after 1844—after Jesus did not come as expected—that multiple "other," incorrect views entered, as denial of the accuracy of the calculations led to repeated new dates for the termination of the prophecy and the return of Jesus.

This understanding of the problem of the "other views" withstands investigation, because we know that at least six times since 1844, Adventism's message and unity was hindered by fanatics who refused sound reasoning and persisted in moving the firmly-established dates for the commencement and end of the 2300-year prophecy. However, the last time prophecy of the Bible had ended in 1844. Believers either stayed on the path established by divinely-led study and prophetic inspiration, or they fell off the path into darkness and confusion.

Having made her reproof regarding date-setting succinctly, Ellen White, in the first sentence of the third paragraph, then moved readers forward, focusing their attention on the task at hand: the proclamation of the third angel's message. It was not to be proclaimed with any appended message of time. It did not and does not "need time to strengthen it; and it will go in mighty power."

In the fourth paragraph of that passage, she identifies one more confusing "other view" being embraced. Some mistakenly believed they had a work to do among the Jews in Old Jerusalem, when there was a more profitable field of labor in the United States. This view she also reproved.

Regarding the actual *definition* of the "daily" in the passage of inquiry, we know that Ellen White could not clarify that term for fellow pioneers because she had "no instruction" regarding its meaning. The question, then, is, "Can the definition of the 'daily' be ascertained from *Early Writings*, 74–76?" The evidence yields one defensible answer: "No."

Yet the proponents of the "daily's" definition as paganism disagree with that assessment. To sustain their view, though, they must mentally supply words so that a key sentence reads thus:

> "When union existed, before 1844, nearly all were united on the correct view of the "daily" [*being paganism*], but in the confusion since 1844, other views [*or definitions*] have been embraced."

Those consciously or unconsciously supplied words conflict with the linguistic context of the paragraph, whose concluding or summary sentence plainly refers to time, not definition, as does the personal testimony of Ellen White herself that her statement in *Early Writings* was never sanctioning the definition of the "daily" as paganism.

The "daily" is *not* defined by statement or implication anywhere in this four-paragraph passage. The compelling interest and emphasis for the pioneers was the "how long" question of Daniel 8:13 and the corresponding answer in the next verse of a specific date, since they knew Daniel's prophecy pertained to their time in history. The termination of the prophecy in 1844 regarding the "daily" and the sanctuary was the unifying element for the Advent believers. Thus the issues of "correct views" regarding time and confusing "other views" involving time-setting that denied the accuracy of the calculations were the focus of Ellen White's recorded vision. Prior to 1844, unity on the actual definition of the "daily" was certainly not as pressing as the event they believed was about to happen.

But in the years since 1844, with understanding gained as to Jesus' ministry in the Most Holy Place, it has become more important to unify on the meaning of the "daily," for disunity dishonors God and weakens the movement. Indeed, Ellen White's last counsel to the brethren regarding the "daily" was to delay no longer to come together to agree on a biblically-based definition for that term:

> "A special work now rests upon us of solemnly investigating these matters, and *in the name of the Lord to unify*." Letter 50, 1910; *Manuscript Releases*, 20:223, emphasis added.

We believe that theological and historical documentation, as well as pioneer correspondence and the records of Inspiration, proves beyond question that the only defensible definition of the "daily" is the ministry of Christ in the first apartment.

As further confirmation of the chronology traced above and its implications regarding a definition of the "daily," we find that W. W. Prescott's published views are in harmony with the historical evidence here presented and with the writings of Ellen White. In his leaflet *The Daily: A Brief Reply to the Two Leaflets on This Subject*, he presented a historical context of relevant events that occurred prior to the writing of the *Early Writings* passage under investigation. His objective was to show that the passage in question could not be used to support the paganism view, because the definition of the "daily" was not even a significant issue at that time in history. The dominant interest during that time period was time fulfillment of the 2300-year prophecy and the post-1844 flurry of time-setting. Again, the pioneers' overwhelming focus was "How long?" not "What is?" That focus indicated their "correct view" regarding the "daily." His written argument is here quoted, beginning midway through the second paragraph:

> "Inasmuch as an appeal has been made to the teaching of the spirit of prophecy as the basis for the claim that the 'daily' of Daniel 8 is paganism, and that it was taken away in 508 A.D., it seems necessary to consider what is said in the spirit of prophecy concerning the 'daily,' in order that, if possible, the prejudice which has been created by the misinterpretation of a certain quotation may be removed. But instead of quoting one or two sentences out of their connection, and interpreting them in harmony with a preconceived opinion, we will quote more at length the passage in question, as found in 'Early Writings' (edition of 1893), page 64 of the first part: [Here the four paragraphs in question are quoted.]
>
> "The reading of this extract will make it clear to any unprejudiced mind that the topic under consideration is the question of time. The application of the counsel here given will be understood more clearly by a consideration of the experiences of the Advent believers up to the time when this testimony was given in 1850. The orthodox interpretation of the little horn of the eighth chapter of Daniel was that it was a symbol of Antiochus Epiphanies; that the 2300 days were literal days, commencing with the time when Antiochus polluted the temple at Jerusalem; and that 'the daily sacrifice' referred to the daily offerings made according to the ceremonial law. In harmony with this view the

translators supplied the word 'sacrifice' in the expression 'the daily sacrifice.' The Adventists, on the other hand, maintained that the little horn was a symbol of Rome, pagan and papal; that the 2300 days were prophetic days, fulfilled in literal years; and that this period commenced in B.C. 457 and ended in 1844. After the passing of the time in 1844, there was an effort made to readjust this period of 2300 years to some point in the future; and up to 1850 at least six different adjustments had been made, bringing much confusion into the Advent ranks. Then came this counsel through the spirit of prophecy, that the word 'sacrifice' should not be supplied, and that, therefore, the interpretation which found in the work of Antiochus the fulfillment of this prophecy was incorrect; that the view entertained previous to 1844 which made the year 1844 the true termination of the prophetic period of 2300 years was correct; and that a true time message would never again be proclaimed. 'Time has never been a test since 1844, and it will never be a test.' This same general statement was made later and is found on page 107 [now *Spiritual Gifts*, 1:148], second part of the same edition of 'Early Writings,' being the seventh paragraph of the article entitled 'The Advent Movement Illustrated:'

"'Jesus did not come to earth as the waiting, joyful company expected, to cleanse the sanctuary by purifying the earth by fire. I saw that they were correct in their reckoning of the prophetic periods; prophetic time closed in 1844, and Jesus entered the most holy place to cleanse the sanctuary at the ending of the days. Their mistake consisted in not understanding what the sanctuary was and the nature of its cleansing.'

"That this is the right view of this instruction given through the spirit of prophecy will appear more plainly when we remember that since 1844 there has been until recently no difference of opinion as to what the 'daily' was, and that the confusion which arose after 1844 was not on account of a change in interpretation in this respect, but because of the many attempts to readjust the prophetic period of 2300 years and to set new times still in the future for the expiration of this period, and for the appearance of Christ in the clouds of heaven; therefore, it is said,: 'When union existed before 1844, nearly all were united on the correct view of the 'daily;' but in the confusion since 1844 other views have been embraced, and darkness and confusion have followed.' The 'other views' were with reference to time, concerning which many different interpretations were brought forward, causing 'darkness and confusion,' but during all that period there was no controversy as to what the 'daily' represented.

"In interpreting this prophecy the early Adventists placed the emphasis upon the question, 'How long shall be the vision concerning the daily?' etc., and upon the reply, 'Unto two thousand and three hundred evenings and mornings.' This period of time and the date which marked its expiration were the subjects which claimed their chief attention, and concerning these matters they had the correct view."

This accounting of the unity of the early movement based on the certainty of prophetic time interpretation is mirrored in an article by James White:

"B.C. 457, was the year presented, and clearly proved by Brother Miller, as the true date for the commencement of the 2300 days. It was published to the world by every Second Advent paper in the land, by books, and by public lectures, as the true date. The proof was so very conclusive that those who examined the point with candor embraced it at once. Learned opponents did not, and could not; show that we were incorrect in dating the 2300 days from B.C. 457. With this clearly ascertained date for the commencement of the main pillar of the 'original' Advent faith, lecturers went forth united to give the judgment hour cry. This was the date written upon the 'chronological chart of the visions of Daniel and John, [1843 chart], published by J. V. Himes, 14 Devonshire St.'" White, James, *Review and Herald*, Dec. 1850, p. 13, col. 1.

Now read the second paragraph in *Early Writings* again:

"Then I saw in relation to the 'daily' (Daniel 8:12) that the word 'sacrifice' was supplied by man's wisdom, and does not belong to the text, and that the Lord gave the correct view of it to those who gave the judgment hour cry. When union existed, before 1844, nearly all were united on the correct view of the 'daily'; but in the confusion since 1844, other views have been embraced, and darkness and confusion have followed. Time has not been a test since 1844, and it will never again be a test." *Early Writings*, 74–75.

The focus of Daniel 8:13–14 was fulfillment of a time prophecy, and the focus of the *Early Writings* passage was time, as well—upholding the accurate computation of time and rebuking time-setting. Time-setting after 1844 was a tragic setback after such prior confidence in the dates originating from a study of Daniel 8:11–14, which, as we know, gave rise to the Millerite then the Advent movement. It was of such serious consequence that the Lord was moved to send a vision to reprove that activity.

To summarize, then, the "correct view" of the daily on which "nearly all were united" before 1844 referred wholly to time. And so did the incorrect "other views" which caused "darkness and confusion." Both views focused on time—the date of fulfillment of the "vision concerning the daily."

The *definition* of paganism, therefore, has no place in this context, and no valid claim of consensus before 1844, either. While a matter of disagreement, the definition or interpretation of the "daily" simply was not yet an issue of significant weight to cause division, being understandably preceded and eclipsed by the predominant expectation of the Lord's imminent return. It is on the date of the termination of the 2300-year prophecy that the Advent believers were in near-unanimous accord.

A correct understanding of the passage in question is one of utmost importance, because a misunderstanding has prevented unity among us. The overriding usage of the "daily" in Mrs. White's phrase "correct view of the 'daily'" is in connection to the fulfillment of the 2300-year time prophecy. The Advent movement was almost unanimous in their acceptance of the calculations regarding the genesis and termination of the 2300-year prophecy. They knew precisely "how long shall be the vision concerning the daily" and the sanctuary was to extend: to 1844. (See Daniel 8:13.) While we do not deny or belittle the importance of understanding the oppressive acts of the little horn regarding the "daily" and the sanctuary, etc., nevertheless, we claim that to construe a meaning or support for a definition of the "daily" from this particular sentence or from anywhere in that *Early Writings* passage is to misconstrue the entire context, purpose, and emphasis of the passage. When Ellen White referred in the second paragraph to "when union existed, before 1844," the "union" she mentioned was based on the unshakable calculations of time related to Daniel's question that gave such impetus and success to the early movement. After 1844, however, the disappointed, disaffected ones who did not accept the understanding that the sanctuary to be cleansed was the heavenly one began setting new dates for Jesus' imminent return. In the confusion, the movement lost some of its earlier strength. The first three paragraphs in the *Early Writings* passage are indeed all about, and only about, time-setting.

What follows pertains to a serious matter arising during the early years of the Advent movement—a matter which persists today, causing additional disunity. The primary reason the "daily" passage in question was and still is interpreted by some sincere Adventist brethren to be a validation of the paganism view of the "daily" is their belief that, as Prescott expressed it in the opening paragraph of his leaflet, those who would accept any view other than paganism "are squarely contradicting the plain statements of the spirit of prophecy."

This very opinion was expressed by Elder Haskell, one of the leading post-1844 proponents of the paganism view. In a letter to Ellen White on December 6, 1909, he began,

> "We have been very sorry to find that the SIGNS has been bringing Prescott's view of the 'daily' to the front, and that Prescott is trying to weave, adroitly, into the reading for the week of prayer this view, so it will be read by all our people. It is not so much because the doctrine itself would be so bad, were it not for the influence it will have on many minds concerning your testimonies. There are many of our brethren who think your testimonies are changed, and can be changed, and that because of this, they are not reliable. That the light you have had in the past can be changed to new views, and these brethren think the 'Early Writings' teaches in direct opposition to these new views. And right here is the worst effect of these new views on our people."

Notice, please, that Haskell did not find fault with the ministry-of-Christ view:

> "It is not so much because the doctrine itself would be so bad." Rather, he feared the negative effect on the spirit of prophecy if that "new" view were accepted: "Were it not for the influence

it will have on many minds concerning your testimonies."

Ever believing in the divine inspiration of her writings and wishing to preserve belief in them, he explained his point more fully:

> "There are many of our brethren who think your testimonies are changed, and can be changed, and that because of this, they are not reliable. That the light you have had in the past can be changed to new views, and these brethren think that 'Early Writings' teaches in direct opposition to these new views. And right here is the worst effect of these new views on our people."

Haskell believed a loss of confidence in the divine inspiration of Ellen White's counsel would have very serious consequences for the early movement, to which he was devoted. He would not swerve from his belief about the "daily" being paganism, because he believed her words in *Early Writings* indicated support for that view. If any other definition of the "daily" were to be accepted, he worried that her writings, so helpful to the movement, would be discredited. And since he believed her words were inspired, how could he believe otherwise—even in the face of documentation proving paganism untenable?

Ironically, Haskell so greatly feared division in the movement due to shaken confidence in Ellen White's writings that he unwittingly encouraged disunity by his promulgation of the paganism view, despite indisputable evidence disproving it. Sadly, division on both the "daily" and the inspiration of Ellen White's writings unnecessarily continues today, crippling the mission and message of God's final church.

Without doubt, her words were inspired of the Lord to meet the very time-setting crisis the early Adventists were facing. And if you recall from an earlier part of this book, Ellen White herself said, during her interview with Daniells, that the "view that had been held and presented regarding the dates was correct," hence the "correct view" she mentioned twice in that passage in *Early Writings*. Both references—once in regard to a supplied word and once in regard to the "daily"—were in the context of prophetic time.

As it was, the mistaken Haskell and others holding the paganism view simply regarded all contentions that the "daily" was the ministry of Christ as blatant opposition to the spirit of prophecy. Such is the view still held by some sincere souls today, whose motives and integrity we do not impugn while we plead that they reconsider their positions on the basis on information here presented.

We humbly petition the Lord that this exposition may serve to settle the "daily" issue and begin to unite our movement to the degree that it can be said of us exactly what was said of the early Advent movement:

> "Of all the great religious movements since the days of the apostles, none have been more free from human imperfection and the wiles of Satan than was that of the autumn of 1844. Even now, after the lapse of many years, all who shared in that movement and who have stood firm upon the platform of truth still feel the holy influence of that blessed work and bear witness that it was of God." *Great Controversy*, 401.

# 4

## WORD STUDIES, WORLD HISTORY, AND THE FALL OF PAGANISM

In this study of the "daily," we have emphasized that our foundational understanding must not be based upon man's words but upon the scriptures, in which we are shortly to fully review several verses of the book of Daniel. However, in 1888 the Lord sent a most precious message of righteousness by faith to his church through two delegated messengers named A. T. Jones and E. J. Waggoner, who also gave talks on the three angels' messages and the sanctuary. Ellen White publicly endorsed Jones and Waggoner over 100 times. Furthermore, Jones not only closely paralleled but also expanded Crosier's position on the sanctuary—the same view that Ellen White had endorsed because the Lord had revealed to her that Crosier had the true light on the sanctuary. As we have already seen, Ellen White recommended that Crosier's article on the sanctuary be given to every saint. Below are samples of those public endorsements for the works of Jones and Waggoner.

> "I would speak in warning to those who have stood for years resisting light and cherishing the spirit of opposition. How long will you hate and despise the messengers of God's righteousness?" *Testimonies to Ministers*, 96.
> "I have no smooth message to bear to those who have been so long as false guideposts, pointing the wrong way. If you reject Christ's delegated messengers, you reject Christ." Ibid., 97.

Only because of such endorsements by Ellen White do we briefly introduce some of A. T. Jones' work on Daniel 8. Although his works, like any other works of man, must be tested by the rule of faith, nevertheless, given the same endorsement as the work of O. R. L. Crosier, A. T. Jones' writings may also therefore supply us with some present truth yet today. Jones wrote:

> "Now let us read verses 11 and 12 of Daniel 8, and it will be plainly seen that here is exactly the place where Paul found the scripture from which he taught the Thessalonians concerning the 'man of sin' and the 'mystery of iniquity:' 'Yea, he magnified himself even to the Prince of the host, and by him the daily sacrifice was taken away, and *the place of his sanctuary was cast down*. And an host was given him against the daily sacrifice by reason of transgression, and it cast down the truth to the ground; and it practiced and prospered.' *This plainly points out that which took away the priesthood, the ministry, and the sanctuary of God, and of Christianity.*
>
> "It was 'by reason of transgression,' that is, by reason of sin, that this power gained 'the host' that was used to cast down the truth to the ground, to shut away from the church and the world Christ's priesthood, His ministry, and His sanctuary; and to cast it *all* down to the ground and tread it underfoot. It was by reason of transgression that this was accomplished. Transgression is sin, and this is the consideration and the revelation upon which the apostle in 2 Thessalonians defines this power as the 'man of sin' and the 'mystery of iniquity.'
>
> "In Daniel 8:11-13; 11:31; and 12:11, it will be noticed that the word '*sacrifice*' is in every case supplied. And it is wholly supplied; for in its place in the original there is no word at all. In the original the only word that stands in this place, is the word *tamid*, that is here translated '*daily*,' and in these places the expression 'daily' does not refer to the daily sacrifice any more than it refers to the whole daily ministry or continual service of the sanctuary, of which the *sacrifice*

was only a part. The word *tamid* in itself is translated '*daily.*' In Numbers 28 and 29 alone, the word is used seventeen times, referring to the *continual service in the sanctuary.*

"And yet, even the 'man of sin,' the 'mystery of iniquity,' itself bears witness to the necessity of such a service in the church in behalf of sins. For though the 'man of sin,' the 'mystery of iniquity,' has taken away the true priesthood, ministry, and sanctuary of Christ, and has cast these down to the ground to be stamped upon, and has completely hid them from the eyes of the Christian world; yet she did not utterly throw away the *idea*. No, she threw away *the true*, and cast down *the true* to the ground; but, *retaining the idea*, in the place of the true she built up in her own realm an utterly false structure.

"In the place of Christ, the true and divine High Priest of God's own appointment in heaven, she has substituted a human, sinful, and sinning priesthood on earth. In the place of the *continual*, heavenly ministry of Christ in His true priesthood upon His true sacrifice, she has substituted only an *interval* ministry of a human, earthly, sinful, and sinning priesthood in the once-a-day 'daily sacrifice of the mass.' And in the place of the sanctuary and the true tabernacle, which the Lord pitched, and not man, she has substituted her own meeting-places of wood and stone, to which she applies the term 'sanctuary.' Thus, instead of the one continual High Priest, the one continual ministry, and the one continual sanctuary in heaven, which God has ordained, and which is the only true, she has devised out of her own heart and substituted for the only true, many high priests, many ministries, many sacrifices, and many sanctuaries, on earth, which in every possible relation are only human and utterly false."
A. T. Jones, *The Consecrated Way to Christian*

*Perfection,* italics in the original. (For the entire text, see chapter 13, "The Transgression and Abomination of Desolation.")

In this excerpt from the writings of Jones and in previous chapters, we have laid down a factual historical platform regarding the prophetic and historical understandings of the pioneer brethren on both sides of the issue. More documentation on that topic will be forthcoming, but already many speculative and erroneous ideas about their positions can be laid to rest so that the scriptures in the book of Daniel can be addressed with unprejudiced and receptive minds.

Thus fortified, we now begin a detailed historical and scriptural study of Daniel 8. We shall soon see if Brother Jones' work on Daniel 8 contributes to and is consistent with our understanding of God's word. During our entire study of Daniel 8:9–14, 11:31 and 12:11, we will focus on analyzing the verses and their clauses in the most direct, simplified manner. We will not neglect to thoroughly address the principal words, phrases, and clauses that are directly related to our study of the "daily."

Daniel 8:8–9 reads:

> "Therefore the he goat waxed very great: and when he was strong, the great horn was broken; and for it came up four notable ones toward the four winds of heaven. 9. And out of one of them came forth a little horn, which waxed exceeding great, toward the south, and toward the east, and toward the pleasant land."

From where does the little horn come? Does the antecedent favor "out of the winds" or "out of the horns"? What saith the scriptures? In comparison of scripture, we find the following:

> Matt. 24:31 "And he shall send his angels with a great sound of a trumpet, and they shall gather

together his elect from the four winds, from one end of heaven to the other."

Rev. 7:1 "And after these things I saw four angels standing on the four corners of the earth, holding the four winds of the earth, that the wind should not blow on the earth, nor on the sea, nor on any tree."

As we will see, the little horn comes out of one of the four winds of heaven, which represent the four compass directions. Since there has been confusion on this issue, and since proponents of the Antiochus Epiphanes position grossly supply words here to sustain their invalid interpretation, we therefore shall let Brother William Shea, Ph.D., writing for the Bible Research Institute, further address this issue for us.

> "The English translation, 'Out of one of them' obscures and smoothes out the actual Hebrew construction. The sentence actually opens with two prepositional phrases. Translated literally the sentence reads, 'and *from* the one *from them*', etc. The reason why it is important to notice this literal construction is that it provides a precise parallel to the gender of the elements found in the last phrase of v 8. This can best be shown by transposing the first phrase of v 9 to line up beneath the last phrase of v 8 with these elements in parallel columns. Such a procedure presents the following alignment:
>
> | Fem. | Masc. |
> |---|---|
> | v8 'to the four winds | of the heavens' |
> | le arba ruhot | hasamayim |
> | v9 min-ha ahat | mehem |
> | from the one | from *them*' |
>
> "When this procedure is carried out, it can be seen that the gender of the first two elements in v 9 ('one/them') lines up perfectly with the gender of the last two elements at the end of v 8 ('winds/heavens').

"In writing his visions Daniel simply broke up the construct chain at the end of v 8 ('the four winds *of* the heavens') and distributed its two *elements* to two separate prepositional phrases at the beginning of v 9 ('from the one/from them'). This is not poetic parallelism; it is syntactic parallelism in which the gender of the elements in the second statement parallels the gender of the elements in the first, or preceding, statement.

"Thus the antecedent of 'them' in the phrase 'from them' (v 9), is neither 'winds' nor 'horns,' but 'heavens.' Since 'heavens' is masculine by gender and treated as a plural in biblical Hebrew, according to the verbs and adjectives used with it, there is perfect agreement in gender and number with the masculine plural pronoun 'them.' It is not necessary to resort to emendations to bring the text into line with one's preconceptions about where the little horn came from. The feminine 'one' of v 9 refers back to the feminine 'winds' of v 9. The text discloses the origin clearly enough: it came from one of the four winds of the heavens, that is, from one of the directions of the compass.

"From this understanding of the syntax in vs 8-9, it is evident that when the little horn came onto the scene of action, it did not come from the Seleucid horn nor from the other three. In the pictorial vision it is simply seen as coming from one of the compass directions. Thus the syntax of this statement does not support the contention that the little horn developed from the Selucid horn/kingdom." Biblical Research Institute of the General Conference of Seventh-day Adventist, *Selected Studies on Prophetic Interpretation*, 1:42–3, emphasis original. (For further study on verses 8–14 and this issue, see Biblical Research Institute, *Symposium on Daniel*, Vol. 2, hereafter referred to as BRI in this book. We highly recommend this book for the serious student of prophecy, for the brethren have indeed done a superb job on the book of Daniel, from which we shall glean.

Clearly, then the "little horn" moves forth from one of the compass directions on a horizontal plane and expands to other such directions. The direction of the compass from which the "little horn" moved forth can only be from the west.

This brings us to another point of confusion. Is the "little horn" represented by heaven as denoting both pagan and papal Rome? Indeed, pagan and papal Rome are counted as one entity in Daniel and Revelation, as others have so recognized. In Daniel 7:8, 20, 24 the little horn (the papacy) is represented as coming out of the fourth beast (pagan Rome). It is a continuation or part of pagan Rome. In Daniel 8 the little horn power finds its fulfillment only in pagan and papal Rome combined. Heaven counts them as one. In Daniel 11, the king of the north represents both pagan and papal Rome. Both are termed "the king of the north." In Revelation 12:3–4 the dragon power that endeavors to destroy the Christ child was *pagan* Rome. However, verses 13–16 reveal that during the 1260 years, the dragon cast a flood of water out of its mouth to sweep away the woman. This was during the reign of *papal* Rome. Thus, the dragon power of Revelation 12 is also both pagan and papal Rome. This will be important to remember when studying Revelation 17.

All generally recognize that the "little horn" in Daniel 8:9 has two phases, yet is counted as one in the eyes of heaven. In verse 9 we have only a brief introduction, in which is described the expansion of *pagan* Rome on a horizontal plane. Her detailed atrocities, including the crucifixion, are recorded in Daniel 9. Remember that in Eastern mindset, effect precedes its cause; in Western mind set, we follow from cause to effect. In other words, Daniel describes in Daniel 7 the ultimate effect: Christ is pictured as King or King of Kings. In Daniel 8 Christ is pictured as Priest. In Daniel 9 Christ is presented as the Messiah. Thus the focus and theme of each chapter is clear.

Daniel 8:10 reads:

> "And it waxed great, even to the host of heaven; and it cast down some of the host and of the stars to the ground, and stamped upon them."

The "host$^{6635}$ of heaven" is the people of God:

> Ex. 12:41 "And it came to pass at the end of the four hundred and thirty years, even the selfsame day it came to pass, that all the hosts$^{6635}$ of the LORD went out from the land of Egypt."

And "the stars" represent the leaders of the host:

> Rev. 1:20 "The mystery of the seven stars which thou sawest in my right hand, and the seven golden candlesticks. The seven stars are the angels of the seven churches: and the seven candlesticks which thou sawest are the seven churches."

In Daniel 8:10 the focus of the warfare of the little horn shifts to a vertical plane, against heaven. We are introduced to the persecution of the "host" and of the "stars" of "heaven" at the hands of papal Rome. Those being persecuted are God's people, described by Phil. 3:20 as having their citizenship in heaven. The interpretation of Daniel 8:10, 12 by the angel interpreter in Dan. 8:24 declares that the power that is to "prosper and practice" is the same power that "shall destroy the mighty and the holy people" of God. We will fully document this application after we disclose to the reader that the power in verse 12 that was to have "practiced and prospered" is none other than papal Rome. In fact, this vertical plane will be seen all the way to the end of verse 14, as we will soon illustrate.

Believing Daniel 8:10 is largely self-explanatory, we shall move directly to verse 11, since this is where our subject of the "daily" is introduced.

Daniel 8:11 reads:

> "Yea, he magnified himself even to the prince of the host, and by him the daily sacrifice was taken away, and the place of his sanctuary was cast down."

A literal translation reads thus:

> "And he made himself great even to the prince of the host, and from him was taken away the continuance, and the foundation of his sanctuary was thrown down."

"Yea, *he*" has been regarded as significant, in that the Hebrew in Daniel 8 makes a definite gender change from the feminine "little horn" in verse 9 to the masculine gender "he" in verse 11. However, after further study, we do not wish to push this point too far. Scholars have noted that a dual gender in a noun can be seen elsewhere without significance. The context and the angel's interpretation of verses 23–25 will make clear the power being designated after we analyze verses 11-12. Also, it will be made plain that verses 11–14 will meet their fulfillment in chronological order.

First, though, we want to establish the meaning of several words in Daniel 8:11. We'll begin with the word "magnified"[1431] (*gadal*). Usage: AV - magnify 32, great 26, grow 14, nourish up 7, grow up 6, greater 5, misc 25; 112 verses, 115 hits. In Daniel 8:25 we have the interpretation of verse 11 of the vision by the angel and it will clearly settle which phase of Rome that does the "magnifying:"

> "And through his policy also he shall cause craft to prosper in his hand; and he shall magnify himself in his heart, and by peace shall destroy many: he shall also stand up against the Prince of princes; but he shall be broken without hand."

Who is this power that magnifies himself and thinks to stand up against the Prince of princes? The angel declares it will be the power that shall be broken without hand. "Broken without hand" is a clear reference from Daniel 2:44-45 to the Second Coming of Christ:

> "And in the days of these kings shall the God of heaven set up a kingdom, which shall never be destroyed: and the kingdom shall not be left to other people, but it shall break in pieces and consume all these kingdoms, and it shall stand for ever. Forasmuch as thou sawest that the stone was cut out of the mountain without hands, and that it brake in pieces the iron, the brass, the clay, the silver, and the gold; the great God hath made known to the king what shall come to pass hereafter: and the dream is certain, and the interpretation thereof sure."

Second Thessalonians 2:8 makes the inescapable connection between Jesus' return and the end of papal Rome:

> "And then shall that Wicked be revealed, whom the Lord shall consume with the spirit of his mouth, and shall destroy with the brightness of his coming."

Therefore, the presumptuous power brought to view in verse 11 that is to be "broken without hand" cannot be pagan Rome, for it had ceased to exist for many centuries prior. The only logical answer to our question of who that power is, is none other than papal Rome. It is papal Rome, continuing until Jesus' Second Advent, that shall be destroyed by Christ, the Rock that is "cut out of the mountain without hands."

Uriah Smith, in his *Daniel and the Revelation*, p. 159, has erroneously applied the crucifixion of Christ by pagan Rome to the following clause:

"He shall also stand up against the Prince of princes."

However, neither the context nor the antecedent of the "he" in the very next clause supports that application:

"But he shall be broken without hand."

The "he" that "shall be broken without hand" is the same "he" that "also [stands] up against the Prince of princes." This is fulfilled only in papal Rome.

Continuing our word study in Daniel 8:11, we next investigate the meaning of "the Prince[8269] of the host." "Prince" (*sar*) often designates a heavenly being (Daniel 8:11, 25; 10:13, 21; 12:1). The expression "Prince of the host" is never used to designate a high priest in the Old Testament. To the contrary, Joshua 5:14–15 clearly designates the "Prince of the host of Yahweh:"

> "And he said, Nay; but as captain of the host of the LORD am I now come. And Joshua fell on his face to the earth, and did worship, and said unto him, What saith my lord unto his servant? And the captain of the LORD'S host said unto Joshua, Loose thy shoe from off thy foot; for the place whereon thou standest is holy. And Joshua did so."

Further study would show that in Daniel 12:1 Michael is "the great Prince," and in Jude 9 Michael is identified with Christ. In other words, the "Prince of the host" is none other than Jesus Christ.

Regarding "by"[4480] him" (*mimmennu*), those of you who have the KJV with a marginal reading will notice that the translators recognized the word "by" should perhaps be translated "from." Turning to *The Complete Word Study Dictionary: Old Testament* (Chattanooga, Tennessee: AMG Press, 2003, p. 625), we quote for the true meaning of *mimmennu*:

"A preposition used to indicate from, out of, away from; more than; after, since, immediately; because of, since; so that; without; direction as southward, etc. Its basic meaning is from, away from, out of."

We quote from another credible source.

"The Hebrew expression *mimmennu* is not to be translated 'by him' but 'from him.' Who is the antecedent of 'him'? Grammatically, the nearest and most natural antecedent is 'the Prince of the host.' This is supported in the ancient versions." BRI, 404.

One day I asked my Hebrew teacher of twenty-six years' teaching experience, "Should the Hebrew word *mimmennu*[4480] be transliterated as "by" or "from?" Her immediate response was

"*Mimmennu* is never translated 'by;' it is always translated 'from.'"

Thus three authoritive sources speak with one voice. The text will now read "from him," as a reference to the "Prince of the host."

Next we consider the meaning of the "<u>daily</u>"[8548] (*tamid*). Usage: AV- continually 53, continual 26, daily 7, always 6, alway 4, ever 3, perpetual 2, continual employment 1, evermore 1, never 1; 103 verses, 104 hits. We have already illustrated scripturally that the "daily,"[8548] when used in the context of the sanctuary, is always the work of the priest in the first apartment of the sanctuary. Never was the "daily" attributed to the work of the priest in the second apartment, nor to anything else in that context.

Now, when one is interested only in the truth, he is not offended if asked to be receptive to constructive criticism. To be totally fair and open, let us consider the "daily's" interpretation from the opposing side, if you please—from the source most commonly alluded to for the definition of the "daily" being paganism. By 1873 Brother Uriah Smith had clarified his position. He no longer paralleled Crosier but defined the "daily" as such:

> *"What Is the Daily?* The word here rendered 'daily' occurs in the Old Testament one hundred and two times, according to the Hebrew concordance. In the great majority of instances it is rendered 'continual' or 'continually.' It *appears* to be more in accordance with both the construction and the context to *suppose* that the word 'daily' refers to a desolating power. By the 'continuance of desolation,' or the perpetual desolation, we understand that paganism, through all its history, is meant." Uriah Smith, *Daniel and the Revelation*, 164–5, emphasis added.

The careful reader will recognize that after Uriah Smith goes through all 102 (103) verses and can find no verse to sustain the foundation upon which he desires to build, he then declares "it *appears*" to be more consistent "to *suppose*" that the word "daily" refers to "a desolating power." Certainly, "appearances" and "suppositions" are not a foundation upon which Seventh-day Adventists want to build. Since there is no scripture support for Smith's admitted supposition, we shall move on to other word studies.

"*Sacrifice*," we already have learned, is a supplied word and does not belong in the text.

"Taken away" [7311] (*rum*). Usage: AV - (lift, hold, etc.) up 63, exalt 47, high 25, offer 13, give 5, heave 3, extol 3, lofty 3, take 3, tall 3, higher 2, misc 24; 184 verses, 194 hits. What exactly was "taken away" in AD 508? Prior to 1844, William Miller said it was *the conversion of pagan kings that took away paganism in AD 508*, and in that year *paganism ceased*. Charles Fitch, Miller's first ministerial convert, questioned the basis of Miller's interpretation of the "daily."

> "March 5, 1838 Will you have the kindness to inform me, by letter, in what history you find the fact stated that the last of the ten kings was baptized in AD 508." Sylvester Bliss, *Memoirs of William Miller* (Boston, 1853), p. 129.

Brother Fitch never got his reply, because nowhere in the annals of history is there recorded the last of the ten kings having been baptized in AD 508.

After 1844, and especially after 1873 and approaching the turn of the century, there came a marked determination among paganism's advocates to place the basis for the termination of paganism in 508 upon more defensible ground. A new, revised view, the second of four unsustainable changing positions, posited that in AD 508, the *Roman pagan state national religion had been taken away*. However, efforts to promote this new view met with equally determined rebuttal. E. J. Hibbard, writing from San Fernando, California, Nov. 28, 1909, to the son of Uriah Smith, Elder L. A. Smith, then living in Nashville, Tennessee, said:

> "But we cannot agree with you that the system of avowed paganism of Rome was taken away in 508, for that is in no sense true" (p. 1).

Notice, paganism was understood as a system; it was organized. Also, the action of the verb *rum* [7311] was still always used and understood to mean literally to "take away." That means, for paganism advocates, the removal or abolishment of paganism as a system. But never was it suggested or so stated, much less implied, that *rum* was ever understood to mean "lift up" or to "exalt." Neither the event nor the date attempted to be linked to it can be historically supported, as will soon be demonstrated.

Next, we'll view a letter to Mr. I. A. Ford of the Southern Publishing Association in Nashville, Tennessee, from A. G. Daniells, written July 15, 1908, from Tacoma Park Station, Washington, D.C.:

"You are aware that there is a difference of opinion among our leading men concerning the meaning of Daniel 8:11–13. The interpretation of this scripture given by Elder Uriah Smith, and followed by Elder Haskell, does not seem to many of our brethren to be wholly correct. They find it impossible to sustain by good history the claim that Paganism was taken away or abolished as the national religion of Rome in 508 A.D. For six or seven years some have urged that this error, as they believe it to be, should be corrected" (p. 1).

Again, the action of the verb *rum* was commonly understood by those leading men and Mr. Ford to mean "take away." There was no controversy about that interpretation. Rather, the focus of the disagreement was the abolishment of paganism as the national religion of Rome in AD 508.

As a final example, Willie White, writing from Sanitarium, California, to his brother J. E. White in Nashville, Tennessee, on June 1, 1910, on page twelve of a twenty-page letter, states:

"If we take the other position that this passage definitely teaches that the 'daily' is paganism, we are immediately involved with many difficulties. Here are some of them. [We will list only the following one.]

"History does not testify that paganism was taken away in 508. It does, however, show that the work of strengthening the papacy was carried to such a point in that year as to fully justify the adoption of that date as the beginning of the 1290 years. History also clearly shows that the downfall of paganism as a state religion occurred more than a hundred years earlier."

Having hundreds of pages of copies of the original letters, documents, pamphlets and the like on this topic of the "daily" from the 1830s to the 1960s, we have the official positions of the brethren on the "daily." Never once was *rum's* meaning of "take away" disputed from either side. However, this new, second interpretation of paganism, of it being the national religion of Rome that was "taken away" in AD 508 [not "lifted up or exalted"], was now the official teaching of proponents of paganism, and was so taught and believed by them, and so understood by the opponents of the paganism view.

We have already documented how the teaching of William Miller on the "daily" prior to 1844 was built upon a platform of error. Can this new, so-called "historic" teaching of the "daily" stand the test of investigation? According to the opponents of the paganism view, the answer was and is one unanimous "No." Willie White and others declared that history would not sustain the "paganism" position advocated by William Miller, Uriah Smith and Elder Haskell, claiming instead that paganism as a state religion fell (or was taken away) more than a hundred years earlier. They pointed to *The Decline and Fall of the Roman Empire*, by Edward Gibbon (Phila.: Henry T. Coates, n.d.), from which we quote chapter twenty-eight in part, including the quote's footnoted source:

> "These vain pretences were swept away by the last edict of Theodosius, which inflicted a deadly wound on the superstition of the Pagans. A crime of high treason against the state which can be expiated only by the death of the guilty. Cod. Theodos. I. xvi. tit. x. leg. 12."
> This law in the Theodosian law code prohibited any further practice of the pagan state religion and the sacrificing of animals except under penalty of death. There was little resistance to this law that was "given on the sixth day before the ides of November at Constantinople in the year of the second consulship of Arcadius Augustus and the consulship of Rufinus. –November 8, 392."

For the entire original decree, see my preliminary book entitled *508 538 1798 1843 Source Book (Preliminary)*, an overview of the complete documentation to be provided for in my forthcoming full book simply titled *508 538 1798 1843 Source Book* (hereinafter referred to as *Source Book*). The latter contains all necessary and sufficient translated documentation and addresses all the issues and arguments pertaining to the dates of those prophecies and more

This historic document proves that the pagan state religion had received a fatal blow and ceased to exist 116 years before the year 508. Willie White and those who stood with him stand vindicated.

In this same *Theodosian* law code we have this constitution of Book 16, Title 10, Leg. 22:

> "The regulations of constitutions formerly promulgated shall suppress any pagans who survive, although We now believe that there are none. . . . Given on April 9, 423 AD." Clyde Pharr, *The Theodosian Code and Novels and the Sirmondian Constitutions* (Clark, New Jersey: Lawbook Exchange, 2001), p. 476. See also pgs. 473–4 for Bk. 16, Tit. 10, Leg. 12.

Thirty-one years after AD 392, we have eyewitness accounts and personal testimonies from none other than the legislators themselves that have confirmed that the taking away of the pagan Roman state national religion had wholly ceased.

"We now believe that there are none."

The *Theodosian Code* reiterated the death penalty on November 14, 435, for anyone who dared mock their law regarding the prohibition of paganism. Ibid., p. 476, in Bk. 16, Tit. 10, Leg. 25.

But let's take this a step further and ask, "What about after AD 476, when the Western Roman Pagan Empire came to its end and Merovingian Gaul entered onto the stage of prophetic history under the leadership Clovis, King of the Franks? Did the Roman pagan system revive any time prior to 508?" I will let Yitzhak Hen, Ph.D. of medieval history at the University of Cambridge, answer this for us:

> "As far as Merovingian Gaul is concerned, there is no evidence to suggest that any of the pagan religions persisted beyond the fifth century, and there is no pagan religion with a 'complex set of beliefs and practices reflecting man's attitude to the supernatural' which can be identified or reconstructed from the information provided by the sources. All one can say is that the condemned practices were negligible fragments, which did not form any coherent system of beliefs and practices, and which had long since lost their original meaning and implications. Thus, there is no justification for talking in terms of living paganism in Gaul during the Merovingian period. Christianity crushed all sorts of religious systems which existed in Gaul even before the Frankish occupation. Those bits and pieces which did survive, were disconnected from their original system, and therefore do not represent any non-Christian religious or cult. They all survived as fragments of ancient traditions within a Christian framework, and they represent not more than a stage of pluralism which characterized the transition from paganism to Christianity." Yitzhak Hen, *Culture and Religion in Merovingian Gaul*, AD 481–751 (Leiden: Brill, 1995), p. 160.

The condemned practices were none other than that which we have already observed in the *Theodosian Code* as having been outlawed in AD 392 and thereafter: those related to the pagan state religion. Therefore, this new, second interpretation of paganism will not stand the test of investigation, either.

Yet some have been led to believe that the issue in AD 508 was over paganism, because they have understood

that the Visigoths were pagans and that, therefore, the conflict in the West at that time was one over paganism. Before we address this issue, we must first correctly define our terms. What exactly is a "pagan"? We quote:
"One who is not a Christian, one who has no religion, Professing no religion; heathen." *The American Heritage College Dictionary*, 3rd ed., s.v. 1997, "pagan."

So we must ask, were the Visigoths of 507–8 pagans? In fact, the Visigoths were Arian Christians.

Similarly, a few decades later, the issue in the East between the Vandals and Ostrogoths (also Arian Christians) and Justinian was not about paganism, nor was it solely a political conflict. It was a religious war, as well, that would ultimately decide the dominance of the Catholic or Arian faith in Eastern Europe:

"It is evident, from the language of Gregory of Tours, that this conflict between the Franks and Visigoths was regarded by the orthodox party of his own preceding ages as a religious war, on which, humanly speaking, the prevalence of the Catholic or the Arian creed in Western Europe depended." Walter C. Perry, *The Franks* (London: Longman, Brown, Green, Longmans, and Roberts, 1857), p. 85. Perry quotes from Gregory of Tours' *The History of the Franks*, trans. O. M. Dalton (Oxford: Clarendon Press, 1927), 2:36–43. The authority on Clovis, Gregory lived from A.D. 538 to 594.

"The Goths were a people of Germanic stock who erected powerful Christian kingdoms upon the ruins of the Roman Empire in the West. Their spiritual life was perhaps higher than that of their opponents, and their moral standards were admittedly superior. They were more tolerant and their theology was simple and based on the Scriptures. After the fall of the Vandal and Ostrogothic kingdoms and the conversion of the Suevi and the Burgundians the Visigoths were the only Germanic people of Arian faith." *The New Schaff-Herzog Encyclopedia of Religious Knowledge,* s.v. "Goths" (New York, London: Funk and Wagnalls, 1909), 5:32–34.

Historical documentation once again validates no place for the paganism view.

This brings us to a third definition for paganism that has gained a large following long after the death of Ellen White. Supporters of this more recent definition began advocating that the Hebrew word *rum*,[7311] "take away," now means to "lift up" or "to exalt." To unsuspecting minds and the unread, this is represented as historic Adventism, while those who present the ministry of Christ view are said to be teaching the "new" view.

Be not deceived, brothers and sisters. Nothing could be further from the truth. We are obliged to point out that, in fact, it is *they* that are teaching something new. In strict justice, it is *they* that are to be charged with departing from historic Adventism.

Nevertheless, let us look again a little closer to the phrase "take away," *rum*,[7311] as found in Daniel 8:11. When the Hebrew word *rum* is used in the context of the sanctuary, the action of the verb is described as to "take away" or to "remove." Notice how this is done in the following verses, please.

> Lev. 2:9 "And the priest shall take[7311] from the meat offering a memorial thereof, and shall burn it upon the altar: it is an offering made by fire, of a sweet savour unto the LORD."
> Lev. 4:8 "And he shall take[7311] off from it all the fat of the bullock for the sin offering; the fat that covereth the inwards, and all the fat that is upon the inwards,"
> Lev. 4:10 "As it was taken[7311] off from the bullock of the sacrifice of peace offerings: and the priest shall burn them upon the altar of the burnt offering."

Lev. 4:19 "And he shall take[7311] all his fat from him, and burn it upon the altar."

Lev. 6:10 "And the priest shall put on his linen garment, and his linen breeches shall he put upon his flesh, and take[7311] up [to remove]the ashes which the fire hath consumed with the burnt offering on the altar, and he shall put them beside the altar."

Lev. 6:15 "And he shall take[7311] of it his handful, of the flour of the meat offering, and of the oil thereof, and all the frankincense which is upon the meat offering, and shall burn it upon the altar for a sweet savour, even the memorial of it, unto the LORD."

This meaning of "take away" or "remove" is especially true of Daniel 8:11, as the action of the verb is universally acknowledged by the following:

"It can have the sense of removing something, abolishing it (Dan. 8:11)." *The Complete Word Study Dictionary: Old Testament* (Chattanooga, Tennessee: AMG Press, 2003), 1042.

While it is true that *rum* can mean "lift up" or "to exalt," we have already found that nowhere does the Bible say that paganism is the "daily," so there is no foundation upon which to build here. And nowhere in any of the annals of history has paganism as a system survived after the fifth century in order to be exalted. And in no way can it be shown that the "daily" is both pagan and papal Rome, which in turn will eliminate anyone trying to build a foundation on the sand dunes of private interpretation by using a false premise wrested from clear wording in *Great Controversy*, p. 50.

We will return to this Hebrew word *rum* to consider the possibility that Daniel wanted to convey the idea of "exalt" or "take away" or both, in contrast to the Hebrew word *sur*,[5493] in regard to the terms "take away" or "taken away" in Daniel 11:31 and 12:11. A few more pieces of the big puzzle must be put in place, though, before being definitive here and before revealing paganism's fourth and newest definition.

As we continue our word study of Daniel 8:11, we next want to scrutinize the noun "place"[4349] (*makon*) from the clause "the place of his sanctuary was cast down." (An important distinction is that the sanctuary itself was not cast down but, rather, the "place" of his sanctuary was.) Usage of "place:" AV- place 14, habitation 2, foundations 1; 17 verses, 17 hits. Those who advocate the paganism view of "place" do nothing more than echo Uriah Smith and endorse his construction of "place's" meaning:

> "Pagan Rome was remodeled into papal Rome. 'The place of his sanctuary,' or worship, the city of Rome, was cast down. The seat of government was removed by Constantine to Constantinople, A. D. 330. This same transaction is brought to view in Revelation 13: 2, where it is said that the dragon, pagan Rome, gave to the beast, papal Rome, his seat, the city of Rome." *Daniel and the Revelation*, 161.

Let us analyze those sentences of Uriah Smith for historical accuracy. Was the pagan city of Rome, which Smith interprets as being the "place of his sanctuary," truly "cast down" in AD 330? Not at all. Smith based his flawed interpretation on a document known by historians as the *Constitutum Domni Constantini Imperatoris*, "The agreement of the lord Constantine the emperor," or better known as the *Donation of Constantine*, in which Constantine allegedly conferred on the papacy extensive privileges and possessions. However, that specious document is just another forgery in the history of the early and medieval church, recognized as such by scholars the world over. Even the Catholic church readily admits to this fact:

> "This document is without doubt a forgery, fabricated somewhere between the years 750 and

850. As early as the fifteenth century its falsity was known and demonstrated." "Donation of Constantine," *The Catholic Encyclopedia* (New York: Appleton, 1909), 5:119.

But the inaccurate historical foundation of Smith's position does not stop there. Smith and other paganism view adherents tell us, as previously seen in his excerpt:

> "The seat of government was removed by Constantine to Constantinople. This same transaction is brought to view in Revelation 13:2."

Is it true that the same event is referred to in Revelation 13:2? Turning to Inspiration, we have this quote from Ellen White:

> "In the sixth century the papacy had become firmly established. Its seat of power was fixed in the imperial city, and the bishop of Rome was declared to be the head over the entire church. Paganism had given place to the papacy. The dragon had given to the beast 'his power, and his seat, and great authority.' Revelation 13:2. And now began the 1260 years of papal oppression foretold in the prophecies of Daniel and the Revelation. Daniel 7:25; Revelation 13:5–7." *Great Controversy*, 54, emphasis added.

When did the 1260 years of papal oppression begin? AD 330 or 538? Of course, 538—hence, another error. Smith's first misunderstanding about the *Donation* led to a second one here revealed. A third error will now be exposed.

Uriah Smith and the advocates of paganism tell us that the meaning of the word "place" in Daniel 8:11 is "'the place of his sanctuary,' or worship, the city of Rome." They claim that in AD 330, Rome was "cast down," thus, they say, indicating the demise of paganism in that year. How was this accomplished, according to them?

> "The seat of government was removed by Constantine to Constantinople, A. D. 330."

While it is true that the capitol was moved to Constantinople, history unanimously reports it was done for political expediency and was not the result of any attempt to undermine or vanquish paganism. Nor did it result in the historical demise of paganism in that year. More importantly, though, Smith's comprehension of the event, based as it is on the forged *Donation of Constantine*, completely misses the true understanding of "place."

So what is the "place"[4349] in Daniel 8:11 that was "cast down"? For purest light and understanding on the true meaning of the "place[4349] (*makon*) of his sanctuary," we turn to the scriptures to see what the Bible says.

> 2 Chron. 6:30 "Then hear thou from heaven thy dwelling place,[4349] and forgive, and render unto every man according unto all his ways, whose heart thou knowest; (for thou only knowest the hearts of the children of men.)"
> 2 Chron. 6:33 "Then hear thou from the heavens, even from thy dwelling place,[4349] and do according to all that the stranger calleth to thee for; that all people of the earth may know thy name, and fear thee, as doth thy people Israel, and may know that this house which I have built is called by thy name."
> 2 Chron. 6:39 "Then hear thou from the heavens, even from thy dwelling place,[4349] their prayer and their supplications, and maintain their cause, and forgive thy people which have sinned against thee."

We know that "by him the daily *sacrifice* was taken away, and the place of his sanctuary was cast down."

We see from these verses that the "place" referred to is where prayers are heard and sins are forgiven, i.e., the heavenly sanctuary. That heavenly "place" has been cast down—removed from men's remembrance by the same entity that "took away" the "daily" *from* Christ by interposing an earthly counterfeit of His "daily" ministration in the sanctuary. Without question, these scriptures reveal that the little horn has taken on a priestly attire and presumes to perform priestly functions. The horn's plain intention continues to be to deflect men's interest in heaven and God's interaction with humanity by inserting himself between man and his interceding Savior and in the place of Christ. It was not *pagan* Rome but *papal* Rome who dared and dares to attempt to usurp the prerogatives of God, who alone can answer prayers and forgive sins. *That* is the significant event paganism proponents miss.

To expand upon our Biblical study of "place," as well as for confirmation of our understanding, we ask again, "What is God's dwelling place[4349] (*makon*)?" The answer comes,

> Ps. 89:14 "Justice and judgment are the habitation[4349] (*makon*) of thy throne: mercy and truth shall go before thy face."
>
> Ps. 97:2 "Clouds and darkness are round about him: righteousness and judgment are the habitation[4349] (*makon*) of his throne."

Righteousness, judgment and justice are said to be the *makon*, the "place of his sanctuary." They constitute the "basis" or "foundation" of His throne. That meaning of "foundation" is also used in connection with the Jerusalem temple, and in one instance designates the whole site or area of Mt. Zion: Ezra 2:68; Isa. 4:5. Of the remaining ten verses out of the seventeen times the Bible uses this word *makon* in the Old Testament, we find in Psalm 104:5 the only instance in which *makon* is not employed in a reference to the sanctuary. That singular usage refers in metaphorical language to God's act of establishing the *earth* "upon its foundations." Otherwise, seven times *makon* is used for the designation of God's "place of dwelling:" 1 Kings 8: 39, 43, 49; 2 Chron. 6:2, 30, 33, 39. These texts show His "place of dwelling" is in heaven: 1 Kings 8: 39, 43, 49; 2 Chron. 6:30, 33, 39; Ps. 33:14. Three times it is used for His earthly "place of dwelling," namely, His earthly sanctuary: 1 Kings 8:13; 2 Chron. 6:2; Ex. 15:17. The context of Isa. 18:4 could allow *makon* to be either the heavenly or earthly "dwelling." Never, though, is the *makon* said to represent a pagan sanctuary or ever even allude to anything of a pagan or of a sinful nature. For further confirmation by Ellen White of only a divine sanctuary use, see *Prophets and Kings*, 41–2.

These scriptures bring us again to the settled Biblical fact that it was the heavenly "foundation" of His throne that the little horn thought to cast down to the ground [earth]. In no instance is this term connected with the idea of contamination or defilement. The horn's act of throwing down the *makon* ("foundation" or "place") of the sanctuary in heaven is an interference with God's hearing the prayers of His people and an interference with the forgiveness that is the basis and foundation of God's sanctuary in heaven.

We now progress to the interpretation of the second noun in the phrase "the place of his sanctuary:" sanctuary[4720] (*miqdash*). Usage: AV- sanctuary 69, holy place 3, chapel 1, hallowed part 1; 72 verses, 74 hits. Let us examine this word's application in the Bible.

> Ex. 15:17 "Thou shalt bring them in, and plant them in the mountain of thine inheritance, in the place,[4349] O LORD, which thou hast made for thee to dwell in, in the Sanctuary,[4720] O Lord, which thy hands have established."

Here we have His "foundation" (*makon*) and His "sanctuary" *(miqdash)* all in the same verse. The Bible says that our God dwells in the *miqdash* of the earthly sanctuary. This is nothing less than "the pattern" of the great original where God Himself dwells in the heavenly sanctuary:

> Ex. 25:8, 9 "And let them make me a <u>sanctuary</u>;[4720] that I may dwell among them. According to all that I show thee, after the pattern of the tabernacle, and the pattern of all the instruments thereof, even so shall ye make it."

*Miqdash* may refer to God's sanctuary/temple in the earth specifically on the great Day of Atonement:

> Lev. 16:33 "And he shall make an atonement for the holy <u>sanctuary</u>,[4720] and he shall make an atonement for the tabernacle of the congregation, and for the altar, and he shall make an atonement for the priests, and for all the people of the congregation."

It may refer to God's sanctuary/temple on earth:

> Ps. 68:35 "O God, thou art terrible out of thy holy <u>places</u>:[4720] the God of Israel is he that giveth strength and power unto his people. Blessed be God."

And *miqdash* may refer to God's sanctuary/temple on earth and in heaven in the same verse:

> Ps. 96:6 "Honour and majesty are before him: strength and beauty are in his <u>sanctuary</u>."[4720]

It is true that *miqdash* can refer to a sanctuary of Satan, while *qodesh* solely refers to the sanctuary of the Lord. But those who are looking for a pagan sanctuary will not find it here in the context of Daniel 8:11. This position will be cemented even further as we progress in our study, but the Bible does tell us the term heaven uses to describe "pagan holy places" or a "pagan sanctuary:" "place"[4725] (*maqom*). Usage: AV- place 391, home 3, room 3, whithersoever 2, open 1, space 1, country 1; 379 verses, 402 hits.

Let's view the word "place" (*maqom*) as it appears in Deuteronomy:

> Deut. 12:2 "Ye shall utterly destroy all the places,[4725] wherein the nations which ye shall possess served their gods, upon the high mountains, and upon the hills, and under every green tree:"
> Deut. 12: 3"And ye shall overthrow their altars, and break their pillars, and burn their groves with fire; and ye shall hew down the graven images of their gods, and destroy the names of them out of that place."[4725]

It is this word *maqom*, clearly alluding to places of pagan religious activity, that Daniel would have used if the sanctuary in 8:11 was a pagan sanctuary.

Again we present evidence that *maqom* is used when referring to pagan sanctuaries:

> Eze. 6:13 "Then shall ye know that I am the LORD, when their slain men shall be among their idols round about their altars, upon every high hill, in all the tops of the mountains, and under every green tree, and under every thick oak, the place[4725] where they did offer sweet savour to all their idols."

According to 2 Cor. 13:1 the meaning of the *maqom* is established by two or three witnesses of scriptures. Without question, then, Daniel would have used *maqom* if he had a pagan sanctuary in mind. Instead, he used *makon*.

Now we move forward to a determination of the meaning of "cast down"[7993] (*shalak*). Usage: AV- cast 77, cast out 15, cast away 11, cast down 11, cast forth 4, cast off 2, adventured 1, hurl 1, misc 3; 121 verses, 125 hits. While the little horn, the papacy, only "thinks to change times and laws," it has indeed "cast down" the continuance of divine services for man's salvation, in that its usurpation and blasphemous priestly claims for centuries have blinded the eyes of too many who knew or presently know nothing of the heavenly mediation available to them. Through church law and through exaltation of the counterfeit worship system so vividly portrayed in 2 Thessalonians 2:4, the truth has been concealed so as to deny or otherwise block access to the forgiveness freely offered. This deliberate obscuring or "casting down" attacks the very foundational intent of God's sanctuary. Inspiration has confirmed this by quoting 2 Thes. 2:7–8:

> "'The mystery of iniquity doth already work; only he who now letteth [hindereth] will let [hinder], until he be taken out of the way. And then shall that Wicked be revealed, whom the Lord shall consume with the spirit of his mouth, and shall destroy with the brightness of his coming.' The prophet Daniel, de-scribing the same power, says, 'He shall speak great words against the Most High, and shall wear out the saints of the Most High, and think to change times and laws.' How strikingly have these prophecies been fulfilled by the Romish Church! . . . The mystery of iniquity, which had already begun to work in Paul's day, will continue its work until it be taken out of the way *at our Lord's second coming.*" *Signs of the Times*, June 12, 1893.

In the eyes of heaven, these acts of the Romish Church to interfere with or prohibit mankind's access to the holy sanctuary are viewed as an attack on God Himself. It should be no marvel that Daniel 8:25 tells us the little horn's interference and audacious claims to the prerogatives of God will end in the ultimate consequence: "He shall be broken without hand."

# 5

## AD 508: CHRIST'S MINISTRY "TAKEN AWAY"

It is in this chapter that we will present some of our most definitive historical and legislative documentation on the "daily." Taken directly from *Source Book*, it shows what really happened in those prophetic years. Finally, the guesswork and debates can end, and Seventh-day Adventism can present a united front on this topic.

We have already witnessed from the scriptures that the "daily," when used in the context of the sanctuary, always referred to the work of the priest in the first apartment. We also discovered that there is no scripture or Spirit of Prophecy support whatsoever for the supposition that the "daily" is paganism, thus revealing that interpretation's human origin. Our accurate understanding of the "daily" can now be applied to Daniel 11:31 and 12:11, in order to fully grasp what is meant by the similar clauses in those two verses:

> Dan. 11:31 "And arms shall stand on his part, and they shall pollute the sanctuary of strength, and shall take away the daily sacrifice, and they shall place the abomination that maketh desolate."
> Dan. 12:11 "And from the time that the daily sacrifice shall be taken away, and the abomination that maketh desolate set up, there shall be a thousand two hundred and ninety days."

In Daniel 7, the little horn attacks the law of God. In Daniel 8 the little horn attacks the gospel, the work of the high priestly ministry of Jesus Christ. The work of the priest is the process by which fallen humans are reconciled to their Creator. That is none other than the gospel work, the gospel of Christ. When church and state amalgamated in 508, as we will soon show, the gospel message of Christ's high priestly ministry in the first apartment, i.e., the "daily," was immediately usurped or taken away, to be replaced by a hellish, presumptuous counterfeit that could not offer salvation. Ellen White confirms this:

> "The accession of the Roman Church to power marked the beginning of the Dark Ages. As her power increased, the darkness deepened. Faith was transferred [usurped] from Christ, the true foundation, to the pope of Rome. Instead of trusting in the Son of God for forgiveness of sins and for eternal salvation, the people looked to the pope, and to the priests and prelates to whom he delegated authority. They were taught that the pope was their earthly mediator and that none could approach God except through him; and, further, that he stood in the place of God to them and was therefore to be implicitly obeyed. A deviation from his requirements was sufficient cause for the severest punishment to be visited upon the bodies and souls of the offenders. Thus the minds of the people were turned away [taken away] to fallible, erring, and cruel men, nay, more, to the prince of darkness himself, who exercised his power through them. Sin was disguised in a garb of sanctity. When the Scriptures are suppressed, and man comes to regard himself as supreme, we need look only for fraud, deception, and debasing iniquity. With the elevation of human laws and traditions was manifest the corruption that ever results from setting aside the law of God.
> 
> "Those were days of peril for the church of Christ. The faithful standard–bearers were few indeed. Though the truth was not left without witnesses, yet at times it seemed that error and superstition would wholly prevail, and true religion would be banished from the earth. The gospel was lost sight of, but the forms of religion were multiplied, and the people were burdened with rigorous exactions. They were taught not

only to look to the pope as their mediator, but to trust to works of their own to atone for sin." *Great Controversy*, 55.

The scriptures and Ellen White confirm that the "daily" was indeed "taken away" as the pope presumed to supplant Christ as humanity's intercessor. Faith was transferred or cast down from heaven to the earth.

In Revelation 10, in the eating of the little book lying open in the angel's hand, John the Revelator foresaw that this suppression of truth would end. Then in Revelation 11:1, referring to the time after the Great Disappointment of 1844 described so vividly in the previous chapter and the additional understanding that followed in its wake, Christ's command was given to spread far and wide the great gospel of Christ's present intercession for us in heaven:

> Revelation 11:1 "And there was given me a reed like unto a rod: and the angel stood, saying, Rise, and measure the temple of God, and the altar, and them that worship therein."

Why was the church then told to take a reed and measure the temple and the altar? The word "reed" in the Greek is *kanne*, from which we get our word "canon." *Canon* means "rule" or "law," or, as Webster defines it, "a standard used in judging something; criterion." For the sake of clarity, *criterion* means "a standard, rule, or test by which a judgment of something can be formed." The Greek word for *measure*, when it is applied to a building or object, means to "preserve" or "restore" it. In other words, we are to use the Bible, the canon or rule of scripture, in our work of examining and restoring the temple and the altar. The temple and altar were to be restored because Daniel had previously said it was going to be taken away. While the Protestant Reformation did emphasize the priesthood of believers, it did not restore the truth concerning the heavenly sanctuary or the "daily," Christ's ministration and function at the altar in that sanctuary.

As we have already seen in Daniel 8:11, the "daily" would be taken away, and the place of his sanctuary would be cast down. The papacy took away the "daily" and cast down the "place" (His foundation, to hear and answer prayers and to forgive sins) of his (Christ's) sanctuary by setting up a counterfeit priesthood, sanctuary and altar. The altar that was to be measured or restored is the altar of incense. The altar of incense in the earthly sanctuary was especially connected with the ministry of the priest in the first apartment. When the Roman Catholic system developed, the world was deceived into looking to the Catholic system of priesthood for its salvation. The great truths of Christ's heavenly sanctuary and of His mediation before the altar in that sanctuary were cast down, lost or, better stated, usurped. Since 1844 these grand truths have been restored to the world through the remnant church. (See Daniel 8:13 and Revelation 11:1-2.) No wonder Ellen White said:

> "The correct understanding of the ministration in the heavenly sanctuary is the foundation of our faith." Letter 208, *Manuscript Releases*, 8:245.

A correct identification and understanding of terms and events is crucial to prophetic interpretation. Thus before we can fully analyze those two verses of Daniel 11:31 and 12:11 and further cement our understanding of Daniel 8:11, it is necessary to establish some background with historical documentation from the Frankish dynasties, in and around AD 508. In doing so, we will illustrate for the first time historically how the "daily" was "taken away," and at the same time "the abomination that maketh desolate [was] set up."

> "Clovis died a Catholic Christian. He had been converted under the influence of his wife, the Burgundian princess Clotilda [a Catholic]. Very probably the main reason for his change of faith was political, for Christianity constituted

a bridge between the Merovingian dynasty and the Gallo-Roman population. The Franks owed much of their long-term success to such strategies of shrewd accommodation. As they themselves were a tiny minority—probably numbering only 150,000-200,000—there was a limit to what they could achieve by force. Thus the Salic laws associated with Clovis were not imposed on Gallo–Romans, who were still judged under Roman law. The old *civitates* and *pagi* (plural of *pagus*) divisions were maintained, and posts of count at *civitas* (singular of *civitates*) level were frequently occupied by the local elites. The Franks also understood the need to have the church of the Gallo-Romans on their side. Bishops played a more important role in local government than most counts, to whom they were often related by ties of kinship. The existing diocesan frame-work was maintained, forming links with classical antiquity that would last until 1790, when the Revolutionaries reorganized France's ecclesiastical geography." John Ardagh, *Cultural Atlas of France* (Alexandria, VA: Stonehenge Press, 1992), 28.

"The Franks were heavily recruited into the Roman army and a segment known as the Salians was settled in what is now the Netherlands. In the early 6th C., the Franks were united politically by Clovis (Chlodovechus, 481½ -511), who extended Frankish rule over the whole of Roman Gaul with the exception of Septimania and Provence. Clovis also converted to Orthodox [Catholic] Christianity, the first barbarian king to do so. This conversion and his victory over the VISIGOTHS (508) contributed to a Byz. perception of the Franks as potential allies against the Arian Gothic kingdoms and later the Lombards in Italy. Merovingian kings from Clovis onward were frequently honored by Constantinople with the titles consul and patrikios." *The Oxford Dictionary of Byzantium*, s.v. "Franks" (New York: Oxford University Press, 1991), 2:803.

"The Church of France was distinguished for many ages by its zeal for the independence and purity of ecclesiastical elections. Under the first and second Frankish dynasties the Church was the main source and principle of civilization—the dominant power of society. All important acts of legislation emanated from its Councils. Its prelates were Ministers of State; its priests were civil magistrates; justice was ordinarily dispensed through its tribunals. Church and State were in fact so intimately blended, as to be scarcely distinguishable the one from the other. During this period, the right of the Church to freedom of action in the choice of its chief pastors was fully admitted in theory; and elections to the episcopate were made, according to primitive usage, by the suffrages of the clergy and faithful laity of the diocese; subject always to the regulations of the canons, and to the approval of the sovereign. It is true that this practice was often interfered with, especially under the later Merovingian princes; but such cases were exceptions and abuses. Freedom of election was the universally acknowledged rule, and was more or less exactly followed until after the fall of the Carlovingian Empire." W. Henley Jervis, *The Gallican Church: A History of the Church of France* (London: John Murray, Albemarle Street, 1872), 1:16.

In the late 560s or early 570s, when the Byzantine historian Agathias was writing the history of Justinian's wars, he chose to include in it an excursus on the Frankish kingdoms.

"The Franks are not nomads, as some of the barbarians certainly are, but actually follow a political system that is for the most part Roman, and the same laws as us. In other respects too—contracts, marriage and religion—they follow the same practice. For they are all in fact Christian, and completely orthodox. They have magistrates and priests in their towns and celebrate the festivals just as we do." Agathias, *Historiarum Libri Quinque*, ed. R. Keydell (Berlin: n.p., 1967), 1:2; trans. Greek, cited in Averil Cameron, "Agathias on the early Merovingians," *Annali della Scuola Normale Superiore di Pisa* 37 (n.p., 1968), 95–140, at p. 105. See also Yitzhak Hen, *Culture & Religion in Merovingian Gaul, AD 481–751* (Leiden: Brill, 1995), introduction. Remember, Averil Cameron reminds us that Agathias is the one to rely on in Frankish matters. See Averil Cameron, *Agathias* (Oxford: n.p., 1970), 50–51, 54–5, 120–21; id., *Procopius and the Sixth Century* (London: n.p., 1985), 210–13; id., "Agathias on the early Merovingians," 136–139. See also H. Ditten, "Zu Prokops Nachrichten fiber die deutschen Stdmme," *Byzantinoslavica* 36 (n.p., 1971), 1–24. Agathius lived from A.D. 536–582.

The perspective of the Catholic Church regarding events and conditions in AD 508 must be considered, in conjunction with the prophecies of Daniel 11:31 and 12:11. The *New Catholic Encyclopedia* describes the issues, motives, and significance of what occurred in that decisive year:

> "Beyond encouraging individual bishops to play a vital role in his kingdom, Clovis sought to use their collective presence as a force to shape a 'National' church that would serve under royal direction to institute a

> common religious life throughout his realm. His entire religious policy played an important role in bringing the Christian establishment into support for the new regime. At the same time Clovis played a significant role in establishing a political and religious order which provided a framework in which the Germanic and Roman worlds could join hands in shaping a new civilization in Western Europe." *New Catholic Encyclopedia*, s.v. "Clovis" (Thomson-Gale, 2003), 809–11. In asso with Catholic University, Washington, D.C.

It was Clovis and Catholicism, the latter being under royal or state direction, that was to institute (according to *Webster's Dictionary:* to "set up" or "place") a "National" church, a state-sponsored religion. What a powerful admission on the part of the church.

And in order for a "National" church to be instituted or set up, a law or laws would have to be in place to serve that purpose. After all, how does a nation speak?

> "The 'speaking' of the nation is the action of its legislative and judicial authorities." *Great Controversy*, 442.

Confirmation of the existence of legislation that set up a "National" religion can be found in the *Breviary* (the *Breviary of Alaric*), the law code that governed the lives of all Gallo-Roman subjects in Gaul. As already witnessed by the historian Agathias and now others, it will be seen that the Franks also came under this law code, including its religious edicts.

In excerpts immediately following, the establishment of this significant law code by Alaric in AD 506 and its widespread and long-standing usage will be confirmed by historians. In Gaul it served Clovis and his subjects

## AD 508: Christ's Ministry "Taken Away"

after his defeat of Alaric, and it continued long after Clovis passed from the stage of history. The inclusion in the *Breviary* of extracts from the *Theodosian Code*, which fact is mentioned in the following excerpts, has special significance, which will shortly be discussed.

> "Alaric II composed, in 506, the Lex Romana Visigothorum, commonly called "Breviaricum Alaricianum," for the benefit of the Roman residents in the kingdom of the Visigoths. It contains extracts from the Theodosian Code and the Novels annexed to it, from the two works of Gaius and Paulus, from the Gregorian and Hermagenian Codes, and from the Responses of Papinian. This code was in force in Spain till the middle of the seventh century. In Gaul the code of Alaric was also in force throughout those provinces, which the Franks conquered from the Visigoths. The Burgundians also formed a code, in 517, known as the Lex Romana Burgundiorum. This was the shortest and most insignificant of them all. It was in force until 536 when the kingdom of the Burgundians was conquered by the Franks, when it was superseded by the Breviarium." Andrew Stephenson, *History of Roman Law* (Boston: Little, Brown, and Company, 1912; reprint, Littleton, CO: Fred B. Rothman, 1992), 106–7.

What is of interest, for our study's purpose, is why Alaric composed his code of law, and what the political and ecclesiastical conditions were at that time. Notice, too, that Alaric, an Arian Christian, undertook his compilation of law in part to "conciliate his Catholic subjects," and that bishops participated in its formulation and in its approval:

> "The sources of Roman law, however, which included the Hermogenian, Gregorian and Theodosian codes, the Theodosian Novels and

the writings of the jurists, and interpretations of law now unknown were too voluminous, their language was not sufficiently clear for popular use, and custom had also made changes in their interpretation. These facts and the opportunity to conciliate his Catholic subjects, who had suffered persecution under Euric, and who, it was feared, might support the Franks in the conflict with that nation which seemed imminent, led Alaric II to undertake a compilation of Roman law for use in purely Roman litigation. This was the *Lex Romana Visigothorum*, generally known as the *Breviary of Alaric*. It is the work of a commission of provincial Roman lawyers and bishops. It was approved by a council of bishops and nobles and was then published in 506 with the command that in the future no other source of law should be used by Roman subjects. In its legislation and interpretations of law, which were derived from existing glosses, we have the Roman law of the fifth and early sixth centuries as it was applied in the courts. A review of its provisions relating to the church and clergy will illustrate their position in an age when the civilizations of German and Roman were blending and ecclesiastical aims were coming to dominate both. The political conditions under which the Breviary was compiled prevented any extensive reproduction of the imperial edicts against heresy. Only two of these in the Theodosian code were included, one in which Honorius ordered the 'one and true Catholic faith' to be observed in Africa, the other his confirmation of the legislation of Theodosius, while the Novels of Theodosius II and Valentinian III, enacted when heresy was no longer a political problem, were allowed to remain unaltered." William K. Boyd, *The Ecclesiastical Edicts of the Theodosian Code* (New York: Columbia University Press, 1905; reprint, Clark, New Jersey: Lawbook Exchange, 2005), 109–11.

# AD 508: Christ's Ministry "Taken Away"

Once little regarded by historians, the *Breviary* is now acknowledged to be a significant historical document.

> "The glosses of the *Breviary* were formerly regarded as unimportant. But legal historians now recognize that they represent the custom of the later fifth and sixth centuries." Ibid., 110.

In *The New Catholic Encyclopedia* under "Lex Romana Visigothorum," the great significance of this law code is recognized. Notice the statement that the *Breviary*, although a civil code of law, "served the church:"

> "LEX ROMANA VISIGOTHORUM, also called, since the 16th century, the *Brevairium Alarici*. It is a code of Roman law issued by the Westgothic King Alaric II in 506 for the Latin population living in his kingdom. A commission made up of legal specialists prepared a draft of the code, which was then examined and approved by an assembly of bishops and provincials. It was abolished in the Westgothic kingdom by King Recceswind in 654, but in southern France, even after the collapse of Westgothic rule, it served the Roman population and the Church into the 12th century, as one of the most important sources for the knowledge of Roman law. The *Lex Romana Visigothorum* contains extracts from the *\*Theodosian Code* (438) and imperial constitutions of the successors of Theodosius to 463, worked-over material from the *Institutes* of Gaius, the *Sentences* of Paul, parts of the *Codex Gregorianus* and *Codex Hermogenianus*, and also a citation from Papinian. In addition, it contains interpretations that explain the meaning of the extracts or fit them into the altered conditions of its own time. While quite inferior to the codification of \*Justinian (the *Corpus Iuris Civilis*, which appeared only 30 years later), the *Lex Romana Visigothorum*

constitutes a significant contribution to late Roman legal science in the western half of the empire." *New Catholic Encyclopedia*, s.v. "Lex Romana Visigothorum" (Washington: Catholic University of America, 1967), 8:688.

In yet another source, the long-standing, far-reaching dominance of the *Lex Romana Visigothorum* is again validated. This fact is noteworthy, for our study's purposes, because of the religious content of portions of that law code.

"In 654 it was repealed by Recceswind, who enacted a new code which was to apply to Goths and Romans indifferently, and thereafter it was forgotten in Spain. In other countries, however, especially France, though it had no formal validity, it continued to be used (See especially Wretschko's article printed in Mommsen's Theodosianus, I. cccvii sqq.), and was the chief document through which knowledge of Roman law was preserved in the West until, in the eleventh century." H. F. Jolowicz, *Historical Introduction to the Study of Roman Law* (London: Cambridge University Press, 1932), 482.

The records of the church council Clovis convened in AD 511 fully cements the fact that he used the *Lex Romana Visigothorum* law code:

". . . *Id constituimus observandum quod ecclesiastici canones decreverunt et lex romana constituit.* . . ."

In other words,

"We have decided that which shall be observed is what the ecclesiastic canons have decreed and the Roman law [*Lex Romana Visigothorum*] has established." Canon I of Orleans I, AD 511.

For the documentation that the popes demanded from Caesar ("the God of forces," Dan. 11:38) the "protection of the one and true faith" in the fourth, fifth and sixth centuries, and for the documentation that St. Remigius declared to three Frankish bishops that Clovis was "not only a preacher of the Catholic faith but also its defender," "(And arms shall stand on his part," Dan. 11:31) see *Source Book*.

Thus far, we have established that the *Breviary* law code, an extensive and complex code of law established in 506, was an important development for the regulation of civil life of Gallo-Romans in Gaul, as well as of the Franks. Its merits caused long and widespread use in maintaining social order and civil peace. However, in our study the *Breviary* has even greater significance because it contained certain constitutions from the preexisting *Theodosian* law code. Those constitutions, which all citizens under the *Breviary* law code were legally bound to obey, were religious in nature.

The *Theodosian* law code, compiled in AD 438, contained three constitutions of particular importance.

## "TITLE 11: RELIGION (DE RELIGIONE)

1. Emperors Arcadius and Honorius Augustuses to Apollodorus, Proconsul of Africa.
   Whenever there is an action involving matters of religion, the bishops must conduct such action. But all other cases which belong to the judges ordinary and to the usage of the secular law must be heard in accordance with the laws.
   Given on the thirteenth day before the kalends of September at Padua in the year of the consulship of the Most Noble Theodorus. –August 20, 399.
   [Interpretation:] This law does not need any interpretation.
2. Emperors Arcadius, Honorius, and Theodosius Augustuses to Diotimus, Proconsul of Africa.

> It is Our will that the edict regarding unity which Our Clemency dispatched throughout the districts of Africa shall be posted, throughout various regions, in order that all men may know that the one and true Catholic faith in Almighty God, as confessed by right belief, shall be preserved.
>
> Given on the third day before the nones of March at Revenna [sic] in the year of the second consulship of Stilicho and the consulship of Anthemius. – March 5, 405.
>
> 3. Emperors Honorius and Theodosius Augustuses to Their dear friend, Marcellinus, Greetings.
>
> We abolish the new superstition, and We command that those regulations in regard to the Catholic law shall be preserved unimpaired and inviolate as they were formerly ordained by antiquity or established by the religious authority of Our Fathers or confirmed by Our Serenity.
>
> Given on the day before the ides of October at Revenna [sic] in the year of the consulship of the Most Noble Varanes. --October 14, 410." Clyde Pharr, *The Theodosian Code and Novels and the Sirmondian Constitutions* (Clark, New Jersey: Lawbook Exchange, 2001), 476. Clyde Pharr lists the *Breviary of Alaric* law codes in his footnotes for title 11 on pg. 476. See also pg. 600.

As can be seen, one of the constitutions called for "all men [to] know that the one and true Catholic faith ... shall be preserved." In claiming only one "true" faith, religious freedom was thereby denied in the *Breviary* law code.

These three constitutions from the *Theodosian Code* were incorporated into the *Breviary* law code in AD 506. (See Gustavus Haenel, *Lex Romana Visigothorum* (n.p., 1962), 252. It is the most complete work of this law code to date, which was issued in AD 506 in Latin. For this same work in German, see Max Conrat (Cohn), *Breviarium Alaricianum* (1903, 1963). See also Theodor Mommsen, *Theodosiani*, for a good reference to the *Breviary* codes in Latin.)

The presence of these constitutions in the *Breviary* law code gives unmistakable prophetic significance to the following historical summation, linked to the continuation of the *Breviary* throughout Clovis' reign:

After Clovis received the titles and dignity of Roman Patricius and consul from the Greek Emperor Anastasius, the diadem and purple robe in the Church of St. Martin, and baptism at Rheims in 508, he was then on his way to Paris, to his royal residence and capital. Henceforth from his coronation in 508, it was the *Breviary* law code that was in place and implemented as the official law code in the provinces of the Gallo-Romans, and also in those provinces that were conquered by the Franks. That same law code remained in use until the twelfth century, as already established by legal historians.

Thus there is indisputable historical confirmation and legislative documentation that the one and true Catholic faith was indeed being "set up," as prophesied. Clovis had become the first Catholic king of the ten divisions of the Western Roman Empire dating from A.D. 476. His ascension to the throne in 508 brought in its train the first instituted "National" religion. All other faiths were outlawed. Then began the long chain reaction during 1290 years of prophetic history, until every European nation accepted the one and true Catholic faith and was led to follow the example of the Franks in using the civil power to enforce the church's dogmas!

# 6

## AD 538: SUNDAY LAWS FULFILL PROPHECY

We have connected Clovis' adoption of the *Breviary* as the law code of his reign to the establishment of a "National" religion—that of Catholicism. In the *Breviary*, an extract from the *Theodosian* code that upheld the "one and true Catholic faith" gave Clovis the necessary legal vehicle to impose the orthodox faith on his subjects. Having now a firm foundation of the historical events, documents, and policies related to AD 508, that understanding must be applied and understood in the context of Daniel 11:31 and 12:11. We'll begin with Daniel 11:31:

> "And arms shall stand on his part, and they shall pollute the sanctuary of strength, and shall take away the daily sacrifice, and they shall place the abomination that maketh desolate."

"And *arms* shall *stand* on his part." With confidence we can say that it was the "arms" of Clovis, the state's military and political strength, that allied itself with Catholicism. (For thorough documentation of this concept, see *Source Book*.) "And *they*" (Clovis and Catholicism) "shall *pollute*" (symbiosis of church and state) "the *sanctuary* of *strength*." "Of strength" should read "the Rock" (masculine singular future tense), as it is rightly translated in the Hebrew. "*The Rock*," of course, is none other than Jesus Christ, so the phrase "sanctuary of strength" can be interpreted "the sanctuary of Christ." Ironically, those who say this is a pagan sanctuary have never been able to explain how one "pollutes" a pagan sanctuary. "And shall take away the "*daily*." ("*Sacrifice*" is a supplied word and does not belong in the text.)

Thus far, three of the four segments of Daniel 11:31 have been documented and interpreted historically. The fourth part now becomes our focus, as a biblical, historical, and inspired basis is sought for a correct understanding of "the abomination that maketh desolate." Note that the "abomination of desolation" is not only "placed" in Daniel 11:31, but "set up" in Daniel 12:11:

> "And they shall place the abomination that maketh desolate."
> "And they [Clovis and Catholicism] shall place [or set up, Daniel 12:11] the abomination."

"Abomination," by its very nature, is sin. It is abhorrent to God, disgusting to Him, "espec. *idolatry* or (concr.) an *idol*." (See *Strong's* #8251, #8441.) In this case, as will be shown, the "sin" is idolatry, manifested in spiritual adultery.

Due to the ominous role of the "abomination," it is prudent to examine that word closely for full understanding. "Abomination," when used prophetically, applies to both pagan and papal Rome. It is employed three times in the book of Daniel:

1. Dan. 9:27 "And for the overspreading of <u>abominations</u> he shall make it desolate, even until the consummation, and that determined shall be poured upon the desolate."
   This refers to the pagan Romans with their idolatrous standards in the siege, capture and destruction of Jerusalem. This is the Old Testament source to which Jesus referred in Matthew 24:15.
2. Dan. 11:31 "And they shall *place* the <u>abomination</u> that maketh desolate."
   This refers to papal Rome.
3. Dan. 12:11 "And the <u>abomination</u> that maketh desolate *set up*."
   This is a repetition and enlargement of Daniel 11:31, and also refers to papal Rome.

Each usage in Daniel is #8251 in concordances and lexicons. It is defined as something that is "abhorrent or blasphemous," or even a "blasphemous activity Most often it is used as a synonym for an idol or idolatry." Warren Baker and Eugene Carpenter, *The Complete Word Study Dictionary: Old Testament*, s.v. "abomination" (Chattanooga: AMG Publishers, 2003), 1193.

Before applying that meaning to pagan and papal Rome, however, "abomination's" six uses in the New Testament should be considered in conjunction with its Old Testament usage.

1. Matt. 24:15 "When ye therefore shall see the abomination of desolation, spoken of by Daniel the prophet, stand in the holy place.."
    The "abomination" spoken of here refers to the pagan Roman armies surrounding Jerusalem with their idolatrous standards. Ellen White, in commenting on this, connects "abomination" with Rome's idolatry:
    "When the idolatrous standards of the Romans should be set up in the holy ground which extended some furlongs outside of the city walls, then the followers of Christ were to find safety in flight." *Great Controversy*, 26.
2. Mark 13:14 "But when ye shall see the abomination of desolation, spoken of by Daniel the prophet, standing where it ought not, (let him that readeth understand)."
    This is applied to the same action by the same power as in Matthew 24:15.
3. Luke 16:15 "Ye are they which justify yourselves before men; but God knoweth your hearts: for that which is highly esteemed among men is abomination in the sight of God."
    This refers to things men permit or seek that are in competition with their loyalty and homage to God—things that God therefore hates. It indirectly refers to idolatry.
4. Rev. 17:4 "And the woman was arrayed in purple and scarlet colour, and decked with

gold and precious stones and pearls, having a golden cup in her hand full of abominations and filthiness of her fornication."
This applies to papal Rome.

5. Rev. 17:5. "And upon her forehead was a name written, MYSTERY, BABYLON THE GREAT, THE MOTHER OF HARLOTS AND ABOMINATIONS OF THE EARTH."
This again is applied to papal Rome.

6. Rev. 21:27. "And there shall in no wise enter into it anything that defileth, neither whatsoever worketh abomination, or maketh a lie"
This is applied to all idolaters.

Thus twice in the New Testament, "abomination" is specifically applied to pagan Rome and twice to papal Rome. In each case, its meaning is defined as something detestable—specifically, as idolatry or idolatrous worship (*Strong's* #946).

And in the book of Daniel, that same meaning is once applied to pagan Rome and twice to papal Rome. Idolatry is rejection of God, defection from His law and His principles, a preference for another ruler—even self—whose influence, power and values are preferred above God's. This is the significance and application of the term "abomination," the particular "sin" referred to in these prophetic Scriptures.

Exactly how this idolatry manifested itself in the "abomination" of prophecy, within the documented historical context of a counterfeit worship system and the growing symbiosis of church and state, can be seen in an investigation of a related term of equal significance—that of spiritual fornication or spiritual adultery. A church can be guilty of the sin of spiritual fornication or spiritual adultery in three ways.

1. By the worship of idolatrous images, which is spiritual unfaithfulness to Christ:
Eze. 16:17 "Thou has made to thyself images

## AD 538: Sunday Laws Fulfill Prophecy

of men [idols] and did commit whoredom [fornication] with them."

By worshiping images, ancient Israel was unfaithful to God: Jer. 3:6, 9 "She committed adultery with sticks and stones."

2. By the church becoming friendly with the degenerate world:
James 4:4 "Ye adulterers and adulteresses, know ye not that the friendship of the world is enmity with God?"

3. By the union of church and state:
Romans 13:7 "Render therefore to all their dues: tribute to whom tribute is due; custom to whom custom; fear to whom fear; honour to whom honour."

By illicit or forbidden union, the church commits spiritual adultery. In Scripture, the spiritual husband of the church is Jesus Christ. If a church unites with or receives favors from one who is not her husband, she commits spiritual adultery or spiritual fornication. That unlawful union occurs when the kings, rulers or civil powers of the state unite with the church and/or support the church's interests and aims. It occurs when the church forsakes its dependence upon divine grace and power, preferring instead earthly power, usually as expressed in legislative decrees. She thus devotes her energies and priorities to a mutual relationship with someone or something other than the One who deserves such attention. It is spiritual unfaithfulness, spiritual adultery, in the sight of God. Her unlawful act is a form of idolatry. (Pastor Austin P. Cooke, with many thanks for his portions of information.)

In sum, the "abomination" or "sin" of idolatry that is spoken of in Daniel 11:31 and 12:11 refers to the amalgamation or union of church and state. That is the specific sin referred to in those verses of Daniel's prophetic vision. The church had committed spiritual adultery and had married herself to one other than her spiritual husband, Jesus Christ. It can be documented that not long after the demise of the Roman Empire in

AD 476, two popes requested the strong arm of the state for the protection of the faith. (See *Source Book*.)

In this study of "abomination" in the Old Testament and the New, in the context being addressed, Rome's role in prophetic history is thus firmly established. Rejecting Christ, the Church of Rome had transferred her dependence, welcomed the influence of, and given her undue affection and allegiance to the state, thereby crossing a forbidden line into idolatry. It can now be summarized that the "abomination" that desolates = idolatry = spiritual adultery = alliance of church and state = Rome.

This idolatrous development and the setting-up process in 508 came about from church policy under Pope Gelasius I:

AD 492 Gelasius I became the new pope on March 3, 492, and died on November 21, 496, thus ending his pontificate of only four years, eight months and eighteen days. During this short time, however, he established the *two swords* theory, which set forth the church's foundational understanding of church and state relationship.

AD 494 Pope Gelasius I wrote to Emperor Anastasius, declaring the theory of the two swords, or two powers, governing the world.

> "'There are two by which the world is chiefly ruled: the sacred authority (auctoritas) of bishops and the royal power (potestas). Of those the responsibility of bishops is more weighty insofar as they will answer also for the kings of men themselves at divine judgment.' The popes did not claim to wield the temporal sword but to direct its proper use. Gelasius conceived church governance as analogous to that exercised by temporal rulers. This juridical understanding of the papacy guided papal theory and practice in subsequent centuries. The two swords theory maintained that secular leaders were subject to the pope's spiritual authority." J. Michael Miller,

> *The Shepherd and the Rock: Origins, Development, and Mission of the Papacy* (Huntington, IN: Our Sunday Visitor Publishing, 1995), 94–5. Imprimatur.

AD 495 Pope Gelasius I was the first pope to be saluted at a Roman synod as "Vicar of Christ." Ibid., 101.

AD 501 (Pope Symmachus, A.D. 498–514) The church council in Rome pronounced sentence on October 23, 501, that no human court could judge the pope; God alone could do that. Thus the pope was officially exalted above every other man.

> "Thus it was that men acknowledged that they had no power to judge the Pope. St. Avitus, Bishop of Vienne, had declared before the opening of the council: To question the authority of the Pope of Rome is to overthrow not one bishop alone, but the whole Episcopate." Fernand Hayward, *A History of The Popes* (New York: Dutton, 1931), 76. Trans. from the French by monks of St. Augustine's Abbey, Ramsgate. See also Archibald Bower, *The History of the Popes* (London: 1750), 2:261–2.

In developing the identity of the "abomination," Daniel 11:31 describes its distinctive action: "that maketh desolate." When church and state amalgamate, the fruit of that union will always be one of force. To confirm this, all one has to do is read the four verses after Daniel 11:31. All too well, history confirms that Rome physically desolated Christ's true church for nearly 1260 long years. By the acts of Clovis and Catholicism, the union of church and state had been conceived in AD 508.

> "The mingling of church craft and statecraft is represented by the iron and the clay. This union is weakening all the power of the churches. This investing the church with the power of the state will bring evil results. Men have almost

passed the point of God's forbearance. They have invested their strength in politics, and have united with the papacy. But the time will come when God will punish those who have made void His law, and their evil work will recoil upon themselves." *Manuscript 63*, 1899; *Manuscript Releases*, 1:12–13.

Once again Ellen White rightly directs us to the foundational issue, the uniting of church and state after the passing of AD 476. The bride of Christ (the church) cannot unite with the state in any degree, for to do so is to practice idolatry and commit spiritual adultery, and thus the church separates herself from Christ.

The facts have revealed that the "abomination" (or sin) that "desolates" was "set up" (Daniel 12:11). What had taken place was the amalgamation or union of church and state. The *two swords* theory proposed by Pope Gelasius I was to become accepted church and state policy, which in turn brought literal desolation to the Christian church. Simultaneously, the "daily" was "taken away" (Daniel 12:11) when the false gospel of the papal mediatorial system was established as the "one and true Catholic faith." (Clyde Pharr's *The Theodosian Code and Novels and the Sirmondian Constitutions* [Clark, New Jersey: Lawbook Exchange, 2001], lists the *Breviary of Alaric* law codes in his footnotes for title 11 on pg. 476. See also pg. 600.)

It is important to note that those from whom understanding of Christ's heavenly mediation was "taken away" were the true people of God, spiritual Israel. When the false mediatorial system was imposed, free exercise of non–Catholic faiths was proscribed and compulsion of Sunday worship was next to be instituted. As error and superstition grew dominant, confusion increased in God's faithful waiting ones. Over time they became so completely oblivious to the ongoing work in the heavenly sanctuary that, by 1844, God's people actually believed the sanctuary to be cleansed was the earth! They simply had no awareness of Jesus' priestly ministration in the heavenly sanctuary until specific light was given to reestablish that understanding. To say, then, that the "daily," meaning Christ's first-apartment mediation, was not intentionally removed, taken away or obscured from human mindfulness is a denial of some of the most obvious facts of history.

The "one and true Catholic faith" having been legislatively established, then, it was enforced by the state as the law of the land. All other faiths were prohibited.

Thus Satan succeeded in turning the people away from Christ (heavenward) to man (earthward), nay, more, to the prince of darkness himself, which indeed brought spiritual desolation to millions of true Christians. Now it can be seen that the one was being taken away at the same time that the other one was being set up. Both find their prophetic commencement in AD 508 (Daniel 11:31; 12:11 and 8:11). The warning that Paul had given the church in II Thessalonians 2:3–12 regarding the mystery of iniquity then began to take on real meaning. And in reference to spiritual devastation, Ellen White adds this particular:

> "This degrading confession of man to man is the secret spring from which has flowed much of the evil that is defiling the world and fitting it for the final destruction." *Great Controversy*, 567.

It is of interest to mention that Pope Symmachus (AD 498–514), the bishop of Rome who reigned through the time period of 508, has been recognized by Catholic historians for one of his great feats. During his pontificate, through ordination, he created "one hundred and seventeen bishops, ninety-two priests, and sixteen deacons," The Chevalier Artaud De Montor, "Pope Symmachus" [A.D. 498-514], *The Lives and Times of the Popes* (n.p.: Catholic Publication Society, 1911), 1:150. Imprimatur.

It was a number that no previous pope had matched up to the reign of Pope Symmachus. A. T. Jones rightfully declared:

> "It was 'by reason of transgression,' that is, by reason of sin, that this power gained 'the host' that was used to cast down the truth to the ground, to shut away from the church and the world Christ's priesthood, His ministry, and His sanctuary; and to cast it all down to the ground and tread it underfoot." Indeed, a host was given him." *The Consecrated Way to Christian Perfection*, Chapter 13.

It is now appropriate to address a common error that church and state had already merged prior to AD 508, a view that would invalidate the prophetic interpretation here presented and supported. Those who advocate that historical understanding have done so by walking away from the text into private interpretation. In Daniel 7:24–25, one can observe that the issues involved in this prophecy do not come about until after the ten divisions of the Western Roman Empire have come onto the stage of action. That means that antichrist and all its prophetic issues do not come into focus until sometime after AD 476. Anything prior to this in connection to this prophecy is immaterial. We must look for church and state issues after this time.

Previously we said that, in regard to the terms "take away" or "taken away" in Daniel 11:31 and 12:11, we would return to this Hebrew word *rum*[7311] in Daniel 8:11 to consider the possibility of paganism's third untenable interpretation, which is that Daniel wanted to convey the idea of "exalt" or "take away" or both, in contrast to the Hebrew word *sur*.[5493] Now that it has been documented what really took place in 508, we can address this issue with confidence. The research of Brother Gerhard Pfandl, Associate Director of the Biblical Research Institute, General Conference of Seventh-day Adventists, will settle the matter most effectively. We quote from his findings about *rum's* meaning:

> "Peters argues that in Daniel 8:11 it should also be translated 'lifted up' (see above). However,

## AD 538: Sunday Laws Fulfill Prophecy

there is a reason for this exception in Daniel 8:11. The verbal root *rum* in Hiphil/Hophal, the basic meaning of which is "bring aloft, raise up, lift up" (HALOT, 3:1204), takes on a specific meaning in clauses with the preposition *min* (from) and a direct or prepositional object. Proebstle has made a study of the twenty-three passages where *rum* appears with the preposition *min* and direct or prepositional objects (Lev 2:9; 4:8, 10, 19; 6:8; Num 17:2; 18:26, 28, 29, 30, 32; 31:28, 52; 1 Sam 2:8; 1 Kgs 14:7; 16:2; Isa 14:13; 57:14; Ezek 45:1; Ps 75:7; 89:20; 113:7; Dan 8:11; all references are according to the Hebrew Bible) and has come to the following conclusions:

"1. If the object is not personal, i.e., a physical object or part of a (dead) animal, *rum* designates the activity of removing or setting aside something from a larger group of which that object was a part (See Lev 2:9; 4:8, 10, 19; 6:8; Num 17:2; 18:26, 28, 29, 30, 32; 31:28, 52; Isa 14:13; 57:14; Ezek 45:1). To illustrate this point I will quote a few texts:

"Lev 2:9 'the priest shall take [*rum*] from [*min*] the grain offering'

"Num 17:2 'Tell Eleazar . . . to pick up [*rum*] the censers out of [*min*] the blaze'

"Ezek 45:1 'when you divide the land by lot into inheritance, you shall set apart [*rum*] a district for the LORD, a holy section of [*min*] the land'

"2. If the object is a person, the activity of separation or removal expressed by *rum* takes on the additional notion of exaltation. A person is separated from a group to a higher status, usually by God Himself (See 1 Sam 2:8; 1 Kgs 14:7; 16:2; Ps 75:7; 89:20; 113:7).

"1 Sam 2:8 '[God] lifts [*rum*] the beggar from [*min*] the ash heap, To set them among princes'

"Ps 113:7 'I have exalted [*rum*] one chosen from [*min*] the people.'

"In other words, in a cultic context [i.e., in a context of a system of religious worship] *rum* in Hiphil/Hophal means 'to set aside' or 'to remove,' whereas when the context refers to social status it means 'to exalt.' Parallel expressions to *rum*, e. g., *sur* 'remove' (Lev 4:9, 31, 35; Ezek 21:31; 45:9) and *badal* in Niphal 'separate [oneself]' (Num 8:14; 16:21) provide clear support for the conclusion that *rum* in a cultic context always means 'to set apart, remove.'
"Applying what we have just learned to Daniel 8:11 b we come to the following conclusions:
"1. In Daniel 8:11, in a cultic context, the object is impersonal. The word *rum*, therefore, designates the activity of removing or setting aside the *tamid*.
"2. The preposition min indicates from whom the *tamid* is removed. And as indicated above, the person from whom the *tamid* is removed is the Prince of the Host and not the little horn."
Gerhard Pfandl, *Evaluation of "The Mystery of 'The Daily'" by John W. Peters*. July 2005, p. 6–7.

We are now ready to analyze Daniel 8:12:

"And an host was given him against the daily sacrifice by reason of transgression, and it cast down the truth to the ground; and it practised, and prospered."

A literal translation of this verse reads thus:

"And a host will be given over the continuance causing transgression, and it throws the truth down to the earth; and it practiced, and prospered."

"And an host"[6635] (*tsaba*). Usage: AV - host 393, war 41, army 29, battle 5, service 5, appointed time 3, warfare 2, soldiers 1, company 1, misc 5; 485; 461 verses 485 hits. Who is the "host" of verse 12? We have already shown in

## AD 538: Sunday Laws Fulfill Prophecy

verse 11 how the little horn (papal Rome) has taken on priestly attire. The only other entity presented in Daniel 8:11 was "the prince of the host," whom we have also seen was none other than Christ Himself. So it should not be a hard matter for one to recognize that the "host" in verse 12 that is to be set over or given over the "daily" is the one and same "host" in verse 11 that has taken away the "daily" and cast down the "place" of "his" (Christ's) sanctuary. Therefore, the causing of or the conception of transgression has its origin in verse 11, by the heinous illegal acts perpetuated by papal Rome.

At this point all we need to do is verify if heaven uses the term "host" to identify a priesthood of believers or a group of people in religious garb, thus representing themselves to be priestly intercessors.

> Num. 4:2–3 "Take the sum of the sons of Kohath from among the sons of Levi, after their families, by the house of their fathers, From thirty years old and upward even until fifty years old, all that enter into the host,[6635] to do the work in the tabernacle of the congregation."

Clearly, these sanctuary priests were the "host," so we find heaven indeed uses "host" in a context of religious ministry. Thus the host of verse 12 finds its fulfillment only in papal Rome. In the context of Daniel 8:11–12, the supposition that the "host" is in reference to the barbarians that invaded and subverted the Roman Empire has no Biblical or historical support whatsoever.

Continuing with verse 12, we come to the word "transgression"[6588] (*pesa*). Usage: AV - transgression 84, trespass 5, sin 3, rebellion 1; 90 verses 93 hits. This transgression is one committed by human beings. Notice how the Bible introduces this Hebrew word and its context:

> Gen. 31:36 "And Jacob was wroth, and chode with Laban: and Jacob answered and said to Laban, What is my trespass?[6588] what is my sin,

> that thou hast so hotly pursued after me?"
> Gen. 50:17 "So shall ye say unto Joseph, Forgive, I pray thee now, the trespass[6588] of thy brethren, and their sin; for they did unto thee evil: and now, we pray thee, forgive the trespass[6588] of the servants of the God of thy father. And Joseph wept when they spake unto him."

Thus far in Daniel 8:11 and in this first clause in verse 12, "And a host will be given over the continuance [or "daily"] causing transgression," we have seen and documented how this scripture had its fulfillment in AD 508. The Bible now moves us forward to a new time period in the career of the papacy.

> Dan. 8:12 "And it cast down the truth to the ground; and it practised, and prospered."

There are two major clues that determine the chronology of these last two phrases. The first is "the *truth*"[571] (*emeth*). Usage: AV - truth 92, true 18, truly 7, right 3, faithfully 2, assured 1, assuredly 1, establishment 1, faithful 1, sure 1, verity 1; 125 verses 127 hits. What is the "truth" that the papacy cast down? Certainly it was the truth concerning the "daily" and the "place" of his sanctuary that papal Rome cast down or obscured, as we have already witnessed, but the Bible has a much wider and all-encompassing application in mind, for it says:

> Ps. 119:142 "Thy righteousness is an everlasting righteousness, and thy law is the truth.[571]

The first clue is that the Bible says the "law is the truth." So why is the law of God introduced in Daniel 8:12? And by what authority? Before we answer those questions, we must disclose the second clue that will then define the chronology of verse 12.

After the papacy "cast down the truth to the ground"— cast down *the law of God* (Daniel 8:12) (thus proceeding in transgression in the fullest sense), it is then that the

## AD 538: Sunday Laws Fulfill Prophecy

Bible says it "practised, and prospered." Daniel 7:25 confirms this:

> "And he shall speak great words against the most High, and shall wear out the saints of the most High, and think to change times and laws: and they shall be given into his hand until a time and times and the dividing of time."

It was after the man of sin had thought to change times and laws that the Bible says he was then to begin his reign to practice and to prosper for "a time and times and the dividing of time." That is, for 1260 long years, this began in AD 538. Remember,

> "The 'speaking' of the nation is the action of its legislative and judicial authorities." *Great Controversy*, 442.

If it can be documented that the Roman Catholic Church had a Sunday law legislated throughout Christendom in AD 538 by which she compelled the conscience of humanity, history and prophecy will have a perfect fit with far-reaching implications. The years AD 529–534 were the time period when Justinian was developing his *Codex*, another body of civil and ecclesiastical legislation. In 534 it was revised, and in the revision we have his Sunday law as it was then to be read and implemented for his subjects in the East:

> "10. The Emperors Leo and Anthemius to Armasius, Praetorian Prefect.
> "We do not wish holidays dedicated to the majesty of God to be employed in public exhibitions, or be profaned by any annoyances resulting from collections.
> "(1) Hence We decree that Sunday shall always be honored and respected, and exempt from all executions. No notice shall be served upon anyone; no security shall be exacted ; bailiffs

shall remain quiet; advocates shall cease to conduct cases, and this day shall be free from the administration of justice; the harsh voice of the public crier shall be silenced; litigants shall have a respite from their disputes, and enjoy the interval of a truce; adversaries may approach one another without fear ; repentance will have an opportunity to occupy their minds, they can enter into agreements and discuss compromises.

"We do not permit persons who are at leisure during this sacred day to devote themselves to obscene pleasures; and no one shall then demand theatrical exhibitions, the contests of the circus, or the melancholy spectacle of wild beasts; and when Our birthday happens to fall on Sunday, its celebration shall be postponed. If anyone should think that upon this holiday he can venture to interest himself in exhibitions; or the subordinate of any judge, should, under the protest of any public or private business, violate the provisions of this law, he shall suffer the loss of his employment and the confiscation of his property." Scott, S. P. *The Civil Law [of Justianian]* (Union, NJ: Lawbook Exchange), 2001. Codex III. 12, 10. Vol. 12, 277–8.

When Justinian subdued the Ostrogoths in Rome on March 1, 538, Italy then came immediately under his civil and ecclesiastical jurisdiction, including his Sunday law. On May 1, 538, Justinian prohibited "the practice of unlawful religious rites," meaning, of course, that only the "one and true Catholic faith" was to be recognized. Freedom of choice and religious liberty were then totally denied and legislated out of existence. Religious liberty was not to be experienced for another 1260 years, until General Berthier, the French civil "sword," entered Rome, erected the tree of liberty, and on February 15, 1798, in the presence of a large crowd, signed a document and officially decreed, "Rome is Free." Banners at that historic event read "Religion and Liberty," "Sovereignty of the People,"

"Liberty and Equality," "Equality and the Rule of Law." Prophecy had foretold that, in that year, persecution by the Roman church would cease for a time and season, and religious liberty would be legislated into existence at the hands of an unwelcome intruder. Thus the deadly wound was inflicted upon the papacy exactly 1260 years later, fulfilling the specifications of the prophecy to the very letter. And thus was administrated the "judicial punishment" upon the papacy as described in Revelation 13:10.

The takeover of Italy in 538 is confirmed in Justinian's *Novel* of June 1, 538, and it is further confirmed in Justinian's *Codex I*, AD 533, that he did nothing in ecclesiastical matters without the consent of the pope. By the end of 538—only ten days into the new year— it was published in Justinian's *Novel* of March 10, 539, that "Italy, the entire West and those of both Romes" were under his civil and ecclesiastical jurisdiction. (Procopius—AD 500–565, a Byzantine scholar, historian and stenographer for Belisaurius, was present during the conflict with the Ostrogoths. He cites March 1, 538, for the end of the battle with the Ostrogoths, and hence the starting date of the new year is confirmed again, in contrast to Hefele's suggestion for March 25 for the starting of the new year. And lest we stray from our topic of the "daily," see *Source Book* for full documentation on all these dates, references and more.) All that remained of the then-known world of Christendom that was not under Justinian's civil and ecclesiastical jurisdiction was the vast territory of Gaul. However, on May 7, 538, Gaul came under an ecclesiastical Sunday law, as well:

### "THIRD SYNOD AT ORLEANS, A.D. 538.

"The third Synod of Orleans, like the second, was not merely a provincial Synod, since bishops of several ecclesiastical provinces took part in it. The president was the Metropolitan Lupus of Lyons, although the city and diocese of Orleans did not belong to his province, but to that of Sens. Besides him were present the Metropolitans

Pantagathus of Vienne, Leo of Sens, Arcadius of Bourges, and Flavius of Rouen. The Archbishop of Tours, Injurious, was represented by a priest. The Acts were subscribed by nineteen bishops, and seven priests as representatives of absentees. In the subscription of Archbishop Lupus, the time of the holding of the Synod is given as *Die Nonarum mensis tertii, quarto post consulatum paulini junioris V.C. anno 27 regni Domini Childeberti Regis*. This indicates the year 538, and probably the 7th of May, since in ancient times it was common to begin the year with the 25th of March. The assembled bishops declare their aim to be the reestablishment of the old laws of the church and the passing of new ones. This they accomplished in thirty-three canons, many of which contain several ordinances." Charles Joseph Hefele, *A History of the Councils of the Church* (Edinburgh: T. and T., 1895), 4:204–9.

It is significant that the third synod of Orleans, France, in AD 538, was not merely a provincial synod, meaning a local one, narrow or limited in scope. The bishops assembled on that date for the specific purpose of reestablishing the old laws and the passing of new ones. They produced thirty-three canons at this synod. Hefele paraphrases the twenty-eighth canon of the new laws of the church with little justice to the original Latin.

"28. It is a Jewish superstition that it is unlawful to ride or drive on Sunday, or do anything for the decoration of house or person. But field labors are forbidden, so that people may be able to come to church and worship. If anyone acts otherwise, he is to be punished, not by the laity, but by the bishop." Ibid., 208-9.

The original wording of the twenty-eighth canon, as it is translated from the original Latin document into fluent English, reads thus:

"28. Whereas the people are persuaded that they ought not to travel on the Lord's day with the horses, or oxen and carriages, or to prepare anything for food, or to do anything conducive to the cleanliness of houses or men, things which belong to Jewish rather than Christian observances; we have ordained that on the Lord's day what was before lawful to be done may still be done. But from rural work, i.e., plowing, cultivating vines, reaping, mowing, thrashing, clearing away thorns or hedging, we judge it better to abstain, that the people may the more readily come to the churches and have leisure for prayers. If any one be found doing the works forbidden above, let him be punished, not as the civil authorities may direct, but as the ecclesiastical powers may determine." Joannes Dominicus Mansi, *Sacrorum Conciliorum nova et amplissima collectio.* (A facsimile reproduction of the Florence edition of 1759; reprinted, rearranged, Catholic Church Councils, n.p.: 1901–1927), 9:19 (canon 28) (1902). Translated by A. H. Lewis, *A Critical History of Sunday Legislation* (New York: Appleton, 1888), 64. See also Binius, 2:496.

In these primary source documents and church law, there is irrefutable evidence of the compelling of the conscience by the church. The phrase "we have ordained" is of particular significance. Reasoning from the definition in *Webster's Dictionary*, "ordained" is "to decree, order, establish, enact or to appoint" Sunday in direct opposition to the fourth commandment of the Law of God. Rural work was prohibited for the first time, thus perfectly fulfilling the prediction of the prophet:

Dan 7:25 "And he shall speak [by legislation] great words against the most High."

As we shall see from the pen of Ellen White and foretold by prophecy, "the papal power cast down the truth to the ground" (a direct quote from Daniel 8:12). The law of

God was to be cast down and trampled in the dust at a specific time in earth's history.

> "Among the leading causes that had led to the separation of the true church from Rome was the hatred of the latter toward the *Bible Sabbath. As foretold by prophecy, the papal power cast down the truth to the ground. The law of God was trampled in the dust*, while the traditions and customs of men were exalted. The churches that were under the rule of the papacy were early compelled to honor the Sunday as a holy day. Amid the prevailing error and superstition, many, even of the true people of God, became so bewildered that while they observed the Sabbath, they refrained from labor also on the Sunday. But this did not satisfy the papal leaders. They demanded not only that Sunday be hallowed, but that the Sabbath be profaned; and they denounced in the strongest language those who dared to show it honor. It was only by fleeing from the power of Rome that any could obey God's law in peace." *Great Controversy*, 65, emphasis added.

Here is the phenomenal statement that fully confirms our application and interpretation of Daniel 8:12 and the prophetic event that heaven declared commenced the beginning of the 1260-year prophecy:

> "*The change in the fourth commandment exactly fulfills the prophecy*. For this the only authority claimed is that of the church. Here the papal power openly sets itself above God." *Great Controversy*, 446, emphasis added. (See *Source Book* for all additional documentation, including the uprooting of the three horns.)

Hefele paraphrases canon thirty-three thus:

> "No bishop may transgress these canons." Charles Joseph Hefele, *A History of the Councils*

*of the Church* (Edinburgh: T. and T., 1895), 4:209. See also Joannes Dominicus Mansi, *Sacrorum Conciliorum nova et amplissima collectio*. (A facsimile reproduction of the Florence edition of 1759; reprinted, rearranged, Catholic Church Councils, 1901–1927), 9:20 (1902).

The parallel is ironic. God wrote His Ten Commandments in stone, and the church, in this council, wrote her Sunday sabbath in figurative stone when she attested to its implacable intention. The year was AD 538; all of the then-known world of Christendom was under a Sunday law.

In AD 538 we now have a perfect application of 2 Thessalonians 2:4:

> "The archdeceiver had not completed his work. He was resolved to gather the Christian world under his banner and to exercise his power through his vicegerent, the proud pontiff who claimed to be the representative of Christ. Through half-converted pagans, ambitious prelates, and world-loving churchmen he accomplished his purpose. Vast councils were held from time to time, in which the dignitaries of the church were convened from all the world. In nearly every council the Sabbath which God had instituted was pressed down a little lower, while the Sunday was correspondingly exalted. Thus the pagan *festival* came finally to be honored as a divine institution, while the Bible Sabbath was pronounced a relic of Judaism, and its observers were declared to be accursed. The great apostate had succeeded in *exalting himself* 'above all that is called God, or that is worshiped.' 2 Thessalonians 2:4. He had dared to change the only precept of the divine law that unmistakably points all mankind to the true and living God. In the fourth commandment, God is revealed as the Creator of the heavens and the earth, and is thereby distinguished from all false

gods. It was as a memorial of the work of creation that the seventh day was sanctified as a rest day for man. It was designed to keep the living God ever before the minds of men as the source of being and the object of reverence and worship. Satan strives to turn men from their allegiance to God, and from rendering obedience to His law; therefore he directs his efforts especially against that commandment which points to God as the Creator." *Great Controversy*, 53–4, emphasis added.

Please notice that the prophet uses the term "festival," the very term used by Justinian in the original source for the heading of his Sunday laws! The original source reads thus:

"THE CODE OF JUSTINIAN, BOOK III. 12, 10.
TITLE XII.
CONCERNING FESTIVALS."

"And thou shalt be called, The repairer of the breach. . . . Now we have to understand what the breach is. Look at the fourth commandment. . . . Here comes a power under the control of Satan that puts up the first day to be observed. God calls him the man of sin because he has *perpetuated transgression* [*Daniel 8:12*]." *Manuscript Releases* 5:45, emphasis added.

For those who would like to look further into the concepts of "exalt," "magnify," and "truth" in their very close relationship to the law of God, we suggest a study of those words in the context of Daniel 7:25; 8:11–12; 11:36–37; and of 2 Thessalonians 2:4, 10, 12.

# 7

## TWO DESOLATING POWERS?

We have come to the last two Bible texts of Daniel 8:13–14 that need to be addressed and defined. We will examine whether the Bible supports the interpretation that the "continuance of desolation" and the "transgression of desolation" represent two desolating powers of paganism and papalism. We will also document that the advocates of paganism have misinterpreted and misapplied the only noun phrase in Daniel 8 that supports the investigative judgment, and thereby have removed the investigative judgment. Upon completion of reading this book, the reader will have more than sufficient documentation to ably show that 1844 does stand firm in connection with the "daily" of verse 13. The very foundation of our faith is involved in this understanding. We move, then, directly to this next segment of our study:

> Dan. 8:13 "Then I heard one saint speaking, and another saint said unto that certain saint which spake, How long shall be the vision concerning the daily sacrifice, and the transgression of desolation, to give both the sanctuary and the host to be trodden under foot?"

"Then I heard"[8085] (*shama*). Usage: AV - hear 785, hearken 196, obey 81, publish 17, understand 9, obedient 8, diligently 8, shew 6, sound 3, declare 3, discern 2, noise 2, perceive 2, tell 2, reported 2, misc 33; 1072 verses 1159 hits. A literal translation would read "And she will hear" (feminine singular future tense, as written in the original Hebrew). Who is the "she"? Why, of course, it is none other than the church: faithful souls. Notice how faithful souls comprising His church are designated in these following verses:

> 1 John 4:6 "We are of God: he that knoweth God <u>heareth</u> us; he that is not of God heareth not us. Hereby know we the spirit of truth, and the spirit of error."
>
> John 8:43–7 "Why do ye not understand my speech? even because ye cannot hear my word. Ye are of your father the devil, and the lusts of your father ye will do. He was a murderer from the beginning, and abode not in the truth, because there is no truth in him. When he speaketh a lie, he speaketh of his own: for he is a liar, and the father of it. And because I tell you the truth, ye believe me not. Which of you convinceth me of sin? And if I say the truth, why do ye not believe me? He that is of God <u>heareth</u> God's words: ye therefore hear them not, because ye are not of God."

It is the faithful from the 1844 movement and beyond that hear and accept this message of the sanctuary truth that heaven calls and acknowledges as His church. Those that reject this truth and hear not, the Bible says, shut themselves out from and are no longer part of His church, regardless of their profession. Great solemnity should be exercised by all, then, concerning how we respond to the truths of God's Word.

For our next segment of scripture, F. C. Gilbert, in his book *Practical Lessons for the Church of Today* (pgs. 606–8), shows the two saints conversing to be none other than Christ and Gabriel. Christ is portrayed as *Palmoni*, the Wonderful Numberer. F. C. Gilbert's analysis is as follows:

> "From the text of Daniel 8:13, it appears that there were three persons connected with that vision. As to who these three persons were, the margin of the verse makes it a little more clear. We can receive still further clearness from a more literal translation of the text. Here is a literal translation of the first part of the thirteenth verse:
>
> "And I heard a holy one speaking, and a holy

one said to *Palmoni*, who was the speaker, 'How long shall be the vision,' etc.

"In the margin of the text where the words, 'that certain saint which spake' are found, these words are written: 'The numberer of secrets, or the wonderful numberer' (Hebrew: *Palmoni*).

"We find then in verse 13: the speaker, called the wonderful numberer; the holy one, and Daniel. These were the three persons in the vision. Now the more literal translation of the text makes plain that the speaker was the one called *Palmoni*; for the Hebrew reads as follows: *La-pal-moni, Ham-da-bar* unto *Palmoni*, the speaker.

"The Hebrew word, *Palmoni*, is a contracted word. It contains the elements of two Hebrew words. One is, *Pele*, and the other is *Ma-na*. The Hebrew word, *Pele*, means wonderful. See Isaiah 9:6. The word, *Mana*, means numbered. See Daniel 5:25-26. So this contracted Hebrew word, *Palmoni*, literally means wonderful numberer. This Wonderful Numberer is none other than the Lord Jesus Christ. See Isaiah 9:6.

"So one person in the vision, recorded in Daniel 8:13, was the Lord Jesus; the second person, represented by the holy one, was the angel Gabriel. See Daniel 8:16, and compare with Luke 1:19. The third person was Daniel, the prophet. There was something about this vision which Daniel could not understand. So the angel Gabriel asked the Lord Jesus a question for the benefit of Daniel, that the desire of Daniel might be made clear. Instead of the Lord Jesus turning to the angel Gabriel and giving him the answer, the prophet Daniel says that the speaker turned to him, to Daniel, and gave the answer direct to him. Here is what the prophet says:

"'And He said to me,' etc. Daniel 8:14.

"So Christ turned His attention directly to the prophet, and gave the answer to him personally."

It was none other than Christ Himself who said to Daniel, "Unto two thousand and three hundred days; then shall the sanctuary be cleansed." Daniel 8:14. By Christ Himself revealing to Daniel the events that were to transpire at the end of this prophetic period, we are shown the utmost importance heaven places upon this prophecy.

Our next phrase under consideration in Daniel 8:13 is "how long.?" "How[5704] long[4970] (*'ad-matay*). The use of the preposition *'ad* (until) and the conjunction *wa* (then), in the answer of the Holy One, clearly indicates that the phrase *'ad-matay* is inquiring about the *termination* of the vision—not about its *duration*—and should read, "until when." This understanding is evidenced in Gabriel's response to Daniel's confusion:

> Dan. 8:17 "So he came near where I stood: and when he came, I was afraid, and fell upon my face: but he said unto me, Understand, O son of man: for at the time of the end shall be the vision."

Also, in a second conversation held for his benefit, Daniel heard the question,

> Dan. 12:6 "How[5704] long[4970] (*'ad-matay*) shall it be to the end of these wonders?"

Regarding *matay*, Baker and Carpenter's *Complete Word Study Dictionary: Old Testament* (AMG: 2003), page 691, states,

> "With *'ad-* on the front, it has the sense of how long, until when."

Note, too, the answer for the question in Daniel 12:6 is also in the context of the time of the end. The end point (termination) is again given, which was the focus of the question as well as Daniel's concern:

Dan 12:7 "when he shall have accomplished to scatter the power of the holy people, all these things shall be finished."

On this topic Ellen White wrote that the two questions were essentially the same:

> "One thing will certainly be understood from the study of Revelation–that the connection between God and His people is close and decided. A wonderful connection is seen between the universe of heaven and this world. The things revealed to Daniel were afterward complemented by the revelation made to John on the Isle of Patmos. These two books should be carefully studied. Twice Daniel inquired, How long shall it be to the end of time?" *Testimonies to Ministers*, 114–5.

This is an important point that has been overlooked by many. The whole emphasis looked forward to the cleansing of the sanctuary and the removal of sin from the universe.

The entire question, of course, reads,

> Dan. 8:13 "[Until when] shall be the vision[237] (*chazon*) concerning the daily sacrifice, and the transgression of desolation, to give both the sanctuary and the host to be trodden under foot?"

There is a definitive issue here that needs to be understood and illustrated that we will address in the conclusion of this study. At this time, though, we will address an enigma that has perplexed many a mind.

In Daniel 8:13 we have three noun phrases: "the daily," "the transgression of desolation," and "both the sanctuary and the host." Notice that the last two topics are linked together as one: "to give *both* the sanctuary and the host to be trodden under foot." We have, then, three elements that are to be understood at the end of the vision, which we know to be from Oct. 22, 1844. However, Daniel 8:14, being the response to the question in verse 13 involving those three elements to be understood when the vision ends, supplies only one answer which is not specific to those three terms, but more comprehensive. Note that the answer is in the context of the sanctuary:

> Dan. 8:14 "And he said unto me, Unto two thousand and three hundred days; then shall the sanctuary be *cleansed*"[6663] (*nitsdaq*).

How, then, does this answer in verse 14 help us understand those three terms? Indeed, the three terms or elements are to be comprehended in and through an understanding of the sanctuary. Here is where the beauty of the Hebrew language comes into play. We'll start with the action promised in the answer of verse 14: "then shall the sanctuary be *cleansed*."

In Hebrew thought, it is not unusual for all nuances of a word to occur in a single usage. What is implied is the word in all its complementary meanings. That is the clear implication in Daniel 8:14. The Hebrew word for "cleansed"[6663] (*nitsdaq*) contains three basic English meanings, all related to the root word *sadaq*. *Sadaq*: Usage: AV - justify 23, righteous 10, just 3, justice 2, cleansed 1, clear ourselves 1, righteousness 1; 40 verses 41 hits. In our study the Niphal verb form of this root appears only once in the Old Testament, in Daniel 8:14 (*nitsdaq*). The more specific, single meanings of the root word are indicated by the texts in which we find them.

Turning to *The Complete Word Study Dictionary: Old Testament* (AMG: 2003), p. 938, we have this acknowledgement:

> "6663. *sadaq*: A verb meaning to be right, to be righteous, to be just, to be innocent, to be put right, to justify, to declare right, to prove oneself innocent. The word is used twenty out of forty times in the simple stem. In this stem, it basically

means to be right or just. God challenged His own people to show they were right in their claims (Isa. 43:26). The verb can also connote being innocent, for God's people, through the Lord, will be found innocent (Ps. 51:4[6]; Isa. 45:25). Job argued his case effectively, proving himself right and vindicated (Job 11:2; 40:8). The ordinances of God were declared right by the psalmist (Ps. 19:9[10]). In the passive stem, it means to be put right. The verb refers to the altar in the second temple being put right after its defilement (Dan. 8:14). In the intensive stem, the verb means to make or to declare righteous. Judah, because of her sin, made Samaria, her wicked sister, seem righteous (Ezek. 16:51, 52); the Lord asserted that northern Israel had been more just than Judah (Jer. 3:11; cf. Job 32:2). In the causative stem, the verb takes on the meaning of bringing about justice: Absalom began his conspiracy against David by declaring that he would administer justice for everyone (2 Sam. 15:4). The Lord vindicates His servant (Isa. 50:8); every person of God is to declare the rights of the poor or oppressed (Ps. 82:3). In Isaiah 53:11, it has the sense of the Servant helping other persons obtain their rights. Once in the reflexive stem, it means to justify oneself, as when Judah was at a loss as to how he and his brothers could possibly justify themselves before Pharaoh (Gen. 44:16)."

In summary, then, the various stem and verb forms of *sadaq* have the three basic meanings of (1) "to put right" or to "restore;" (2) "to cleanse;" (as we will illustrate) or (3) "to vindicate." With this Biblical understanding and foundation, we are ready to analyze those three noun phrases in Daniel 8:13.

The first of the noun phrases that was to be understood at the end of the vision is "the daily"[8548] (*tamid*). Usage: AV - continually 53, continual 26, daily 7, always 6, alway 4, ever 3, perpetual 2, continual employment 1, evermore 1, never 1; 103 verses 104 hits. We have already documented that the "daily" (*tamid*), when used in the context of the sanctuary, always referred to the work of the priest in the first apartment of the sanctuary.

We have also already demonstrated how the little horn usurped the prerogatives of God, and how and when the "daily" was restored to His church and to the inhabitants of the earth in the renewed knowledge of Christ's work in the sanctuary above. Remember, we have only three main word uses of *sadaq* that can be applied to these three noun phrases for their interpretation. "The daily," the first of those noun phrases included in the question of Daniel 8:13, has to be either (1) "restored" or "set right" since 1844; (2) "cleansed" since 1844; or (3) "vindicated" since 1844. Was the sanctuary and the work of Christ's priestly ministry "restored" or "set right" before the inhabitants of the earth after the passing of Oct. 22, 1844? Yes. Knowledge and understanding of Christ's "continual" heavenly mediation was reestablished or "restored" to believers after that time.

To substantiate that claim from the Bible, we are now going to reiterate an aspect we documented earlier that we feel is absolutely essential for the reader to fully grasp. By repeating this short section within the context of our current study, its significance and application will become clear:

In Revelation 10, in the eating of the little book lying open in the angel's hand, John the Revelator foresaw that suppression of truth would end. Then in Revelation 11:1, referring to post-1844, Christ's command was given to spread the great gospel of Christ's present intercession for us in heaven:

> Rev. 11:1 "And there was given me a reed like unto a rod: and the angel stood, saying, Rise, and measure the temple of God, and the altar."

Why was the church then told to take a reed and measure the temple and the altar? "Reed," in the Greek, is *kanne*, from which we get our word "canon." *Canon* means "rule" or "law," or, as Webster defines it, "a standard used in judging something; criterion." *Criterion* means "a standard, rule, or test by which a judgment of something can be formed." The Greek word for *measure*, applied to a building or object, means to "preserve" or "restore" it. In other words, we are to use the Bible, the canon or rule of scripture, in our work of examining and restoring the temple and the altar. Revelation 11:1 tells us the temple and altar were to be restored to the knowledge of God's people; Daniel 8:11 had prophesied that aspect of the gospel would be "taken away."

The Protestant Reformation accomplished much, but it did not restore the truth concerning the heavenly sanctuary or the "daily," that is, Christ's ministration and function at the altar in that sanctuary. The papacy took away the "daily" and cast down the "place" (His foundation, to hear and answer prayers and to forgive sins) of his (Christ's) sanctuary, or "temple," by setting up a counterfeit priesthood, sanctuary and altar. The altar that was to be measured or restored is the altar of incense. That altar in the earthly sanctuary was especially connected with the ministry of the priest in the first apartment. When the Roman Catholic system developed, the world was deceived into looking to the Catholic system of priesthood for its salvation. The great truths of Christ's heavenly sanctuary and of His mediation before the altar in that sanctuary were cast down, lost or, better stated, usurped (see *Great Controversy*, 55). Since 1844 these grand truths have been restored to the world through the remnant church. (See Daniel 8:13 and Revelation 11:1–2.) No wonder Ellen White said:

> "The correct understanding of the ministration in the heavenly sanctuary is the foundation of our faith." Letter 208, *Manuscript Releases*, 8:245.

Thus we have a prophetic application with a perfect historical fulfillment.

Nevertheless, to be totally equitable, let us theoretically render the "daily" as paganism. Given the only three interpretations for "cleansed" to be applied to those noun phrases, "the daily" being the first of them, we then naturally ask, "Was paganism "restored" or "set right" in 1844?" No. "Was paganism "cleansed" in 1844?" No. "Was paganism "vindicated" in 1844?" No, absolutely not. Thus for the paganism view, there is neither historical nor biblical substantiation for any of those *sadaq* verb applications.

In fact, the focus on paganism sadly results in the failure to apprehend the power and inherent expectation in the true interpretation involving the heavenly sanctuary. The paganism view focuses on the controversy between pagan and papal Rome. It has an earthly, human-to-human or "horizontal" focus. In contrast, the ministry of Christ view has a "vertical" emphasis, revealing an approaching cosmic showdown, namely, the end of the great controversy between Christ and Satan. This controversy is depicted in every chapter of Daniel. One is led to conclude that to continue to proclaim the "daily" as paganism is to deny the veracity of the scriptures and the integrity of Ellen White, to close one's eyes to the facts of history, and to subvert the unity that Christ prayed for in John 17.

We turn our attention now to the second noun phrase under discussion in Daniel 8:13, one that especially prompted us to address this issue in the first place: "the transgression of desolation." The misinterpretation of the "daily" has unfortunately led to a second misinterpretation, that of the "transgression of desolation." Knowing what we know, we could not allow our brothers and sisters to face a courtroom misinformed and unprepared, should they be so required to answer for their faith. Through reasoning together, we also hope for unity among believers.

> "In union there is strength; in division there is weakness and defeat." *Our High Calling*, 170.

Simply put, paganism advocates mainly point back to Uriah Smith's *Daniel and the Revelation*, 164–5, for their meaning and interpretation of "the daily" and the "transgression of desolation." They declare that these two noun phrases represent two desolating powers, the "daily desolation" representing paganism through all its history, and the "transgression of desolation" representing the papal form through all its history. But there is no biblical or Spirit of Prophecy evidence to be found for such assertions.

Ellen White wrote,

> "The Bible must not be interpreted to suit the ideas of men, however long they may have held these ideas to be true. We are not to accept the opinion of commentators as the voice of God; they were erring mortals like ourselves. God has given reasoning powers to us as well as to them. We should make the Bible its own expositor." *Testimonies to Ministers*, 106.

And she called this rule of interpretation by William Miller "simple but intelligent and important:"

> "Scripture must be its own expositor, since it is a rule of itself. If I depend on a teacher to expound it to me then his guessing, desire, creed or wisdom is my rule, not the Bible." *Review and Herald*, November 25, 1884.

Unfortunately, never once has any advocate of the paganism position—from its conception in the early 1800s to the present day—presented his or her biblical or Spirit of Prophecy support to back the claim that the "transgression of desolation" is the papal desolating power.

To verify that claim for ourselves, we have combed through all ninety verses and ninety-three hits on the word "transgression"[6588] (*pesa*). Usage: AV - transgression 84, trespass 5, sin 3, rebellion 1; 90 verses 93hits. We have done the same with all eighty-five verses and eighty-nine hits on the word "desolation"[8074] (*shamem*). Usage: AV - desolate 49, astonished 20, desolation 7, waste 5, destroy 3, wondered 2, amazed 1, astonishment 1, misc

4; 85 verses 92 hits. Nor have we neglected to check all 103 verses and 104 hits on the word "daily."[8548] We have looked in vain for that scripture support. Nowhere throughout the entire Bible is there support for an interpretation of either a pagan or a papal desolating power. No exegetical foundations have been proposed. One is left with the stark reality of their speculative human origin.

The second noun phrase in the question to be understood in the question of Daniel 8:13 is "transgression of desolation." Rightly translated from the Hebrew, "the transgression of desolation" is "the transgression causing horror." (S. R. Driver, D.D., *The Book of Daniel*. Cambridge University Press: 1922, pgs. 118, 150–1, 205–6.)

"Transgression"[6588] is *pesa*. Usage: AV - transgression 84, trespass 5, sin 3, rebellion 1; 90 verses 93 hits. What is the "transgression that causeth horror"? Turning again to the scriptures for our answer, we will see that the "transgression"[6588] (*pesa*) is connected with God's people:

> Dan. 9:24 "Seventy weeks are determined upon thy people and upon thy holy city, to finish the transgression[6588] (*pesa*), and to make an end of sins, and to make reconciliation for iniquity, and to bring in everlasting righteousness, and to seal up the vision and prophecy, and to anoint the most Holy."

The connection between transgression and God's faithful will be confirmed again in Leviticus 16. This side of the Second Coming, the only thing that needs to be cleansed in the heavenly sanctuary on the Day of Atonement is the confessed sins and transgressions of God's people that have gone beforehand to the judgment (1 Timothy 5:24):

> Lev. 16:16, 21 "And he shall make an atonement for the holy place, because of the uncleanness of the children of Israel, and because of their

transgressions⁶⁵⁸⁸ (pesa) in all their sins: and so shall he do for the tabernacle of the congregation, that remaineth among them in the midst of their uncleanness."

"And Aaron shall lay both his hands upon the head of the live goat, and confess over him all the iniquities of the children of Israel, and all their transgressions⁶⁵⁸⁸ (*pesa*) in all their sins, putting them upon the head of the goat, and shall send him away by the hand of a fit man into the wilderness."

Thus the *pesa* ("transgressions" or "sin"), as we have seen, is connected with God's people, and it's also inextricably linked to the heavenly sanctuary.

"This word primarily expresses a rebellion against God and His laws. In addition to the act of transgression itself, this term can also be used to convey the guilt that comes from the transgression (Dan. 8:12, 13; 9:24); or the offering that is presented to atone for the transgression (Mic. 6:7)." Warren Baker and Eugene Carpenter, *The Complete Word Study Dictionary: Old Testament* (Chattanooga: AMG, 2003), 927.

Since the sins of God's people have been transferred to the sanctuary, the sanctuary must be "cleansed" of its accumulated *pesa* before the atonement can be considered complete.

It should be clear to all that the so-called papal desolating power was not "restored" in 1844, nor was it "cleansed" in 1844; nor was it "vindicated" in 1844.

Let us now apply the same three verbs to the "sin" interpretation of "transgression of desolation," to see if it will stand the test of investigation. Was the "transgression of desolation" to be "restored," "cleansed," or "vindicated"? Indeed, "transgression" or sin will be cleansed forever from the heavenly sanctuary and from heaven's books of record of God's people.

A major point of concern presents itself in this context. In declaring that Daniel 8:13's "transgression of desolation" is the papal desolation, the advocates of paganism have thereby misinterpreted and misapplied the only noun phrase in Daniel chapter 8 that proves the investigative judgment. To explain and prove our point, we will begin with a comment from the pen of Ellen White:

> "The term 'sanctuary,' as used in the Bible, refers, first, to the tabernacle built by Moses, as a pattern of heavenly things; and, secondly, to the 'true tabernacle' in heaven, to which the earthly sanctuary pointed. At the death of Christ the typical service ended. The 'true tabernacle' in heaven is the sanctuary of the new covenant. And as the prophecy of Daniel 8:14 is fulfilled in this dispensation, the sanctuary to which it refers must be the sanctuary of the new covenant. At the termination of the 2300 days, in 1844, there had been no sanctuary on earth for many centuries. Thus the prophecy, 'Unto two thousand and three hundred days; then shall the sanctuary be cleansed,' unquestionably points to the sanctuary in heaven." *Great Controversy*, 417.

In Daniel 8, then, the actual cleansing of the sanctuary is referred to only in the noun phrase "transgression of desolation." When paganism adherents connect "transgression of desolation" to a papal desolating power, the true and necessary understanding of investigative judgment is subverted, and the reader is diverted from a vertical plane to that of a horizontal. The true Biblical concept of the investigative judgment, foretold in the language of "transgression of desolation," has been removed and replaced with an earthly entity when, in fact, it is a timely heavenly event of universal import and eternal weight.

It is appropriate now to study two particular Hebrew words that often arise in discussions of Daniel 8. In languages in general, and in the Hebrew language in particular, the context determines which word to use when several words have closely related meanings, or when one word may have more than one meaning. In Daniel 8:13–14, the word used for "sanctuary"[6944] is *qodes*. Usage: AV - holy 262, sanctuary 68, (holy, hallowed,) things 52, most 44, holiness 30, dedicated 5, hallowed 3, consecrated 1, misc 3; 382 verses 470 hits. *Qodes*[6944] can refer to either the first or second apartment of the sanctuary, as Ex. 26:33–34 and numerous other scriptures illustrate.

In regard to the word "sanctuary" in Daniel 8, the shift from *miqdas* in verses 11–12 to *qodes* in verses 13–14 of Daniel 8 comes about because *qodes* is the key term used in Leviticus 16:16, 19, and 30 relative to the "cleansing" of the sanctuary on the Day of Atonement. In other words, when the context regarding the sanctuary deals with "cleansing," *qodes* is always used. The reader will also find that *qodes*[6944] is another terminological link between itself and Leviticus 16, as *qodes* is used no less than seven times in Leviticus 16 to designate the Most Holy Place. See Lev. 16:2–3, 16–17, 20, 23, 27. As an added point of interest, we point out that the Hebrew word *miqdas*[4720] is used as the "sanctuary" in Lev.16:33, but it is rendered "the holy[6944] sanctuary"[4720] (literally, *qodes miqdas*), clearly designating the sanctuary of the Lord.

Daniel 9:24 illustrates the timing and anointing of "the most Holy"[6944] (*qodes*). This major event was to transpire at the end of the seventy weeks. We know the end of the seventy weeks took place in AD 34. Thus the heavenly sanctuary was to be anointed in a very special way at that time. When Christ ascended from the earth to become our great High Priest in the heavenly sanctuary, it was for the purpose of administering its benefits in behalf of humanity. The event that marked the anointing of that sanctuary in heaven was the descent of the Holy Spirit, better known as Pentecost. See Acts 2:14–16; 5:31–32. The anointing of the sanctuary was a prerequisite for its intended use. See Ex. 30:26; 40:9–15. Hence, Daniel 8:13–14 foreshadows the termination of the anointing of the heavenly sanctuary by the initiation of the cleansing of that same sanctuary.

It should be noted by all that, of the three basic word meanings for *sadaq* (*nitsdaq*), Ellen White agrees with the word "cleansed" as heaven's primary focus to be conveyed to the reader. This is in harmony with the Septuagint and the Theodotion, the oldest manuscripts of Daniel written in the Greek. They translate *nitsdaq* as "shall be cleansed."

*Sadaq* is associated with cleansing in at least two other scriptures, as well. The first:

> Job 15:14 "What is man, that he should be clean[2135]? And he which is born of a woman, that he should be righteous[6663]?"

"Clean"[2135] (*zakah*), i.e., "to be innocent: –be (make) clean, cleanse, be clear, count pure," is equated with "righteous"[6663] (*sadaq*), translated "to be (causat. make) right (in a moral or forensic sense):–cleanse, clear self, (be, do) just (-ice, -ify, –ify self)." Briefly, *zakah* ("innocent, clean, cleansed") is paralleled with *sadaq*, which can also mean "cleansed."

In Job 4:17, another parallelism presents the same pairing of meaning.

> Job 4:17 "Shall mortal man be more just[6663] than God? Shall a man be more pure[2891] than his maker?"

"Just"[6663] (*sadaq*) is equated with "pure"[2891] (*taher*), i.e., "morally innocent or holy:–be (make, make self, pronounce) clean, cleanse."

So what was to be cleansed in the heavenly sanctuary in 1844?

> "The ministration of the earthly sanctuary consisted of two divisions; the priests ministered daily in the holy place, while once a year the high priest performed a special work of atonement in

the most holy, for the cleansing of the sanctuary. Day by day [continual, continually] the repentant sinner brought his offering to the door of the tabernacle and, placing his hand upon the victim's head, confessed his sins, thus in figure transferring them from himself to the innocent sacrifice. Such was the work that went on, day by day [continual, continually], throughout the year. The sins of Israel were thus transferred to the sanctuary, and a special work became necessary for their removal." *Great Controversy*, 418.

"Daily," day by day, continually, the repentant sinner brought his offering for his sin to the door of the tabernacle of the first apartment, but once a year a special work in the second apartment became necessary for the removal of the accumulated sins of Israel on the Day of Atonement. While the "daily" ritual involved the cleansing or restoring of the individual, the yearly involved the cleansing of the sanctuary. The point not to be missed here was the necessity of the removal of the aggregate confessed sins of Israel. What is "sin"?

"Our only definition of sin is that given in the word of God; it is 'the transgression of the law.'[1 John 3:4]." *Great Controversy*, 493.

The implications of Daniel 8:13–14 are clearly cosmic in their scope. To misinterpret the message of those verses by suggesting that the "daily" and "transgression of desolation" are referring to anti-God desolating powers is entirely unwarranted, as well as unscriptural. Such interpretations totally miss the spiritual and universal ramifications involved. By so interpreting, paganism advocates have misapplied the only words in Daniel 8 that point forward to the investigative judgment beginning in 1844. God forbid that we hold any longer to tradition and unscriptural teachings, or misrepresent this solemn message of the sanctuary to the world and to our fellow church members.

# 8

# THE "TREADING DOWN" OF THE SANCTUARY AND HOST

Had William Miller and the brethren understood aright the *ha tamid*, the "daily" work of Christ in the heavenly sanctuary, there would never have been a Midnight Cry. In turn, the prophecy of Revelation 10 would never have had its fulfillment. But the Millerites should not be held in contempt for their lack of perception. As we have seen, Daniel had declared the "daily" was to be taken away, and history confirms it was largely removed from the mindfulness of God's people. By the 1840s nearly all believed that the sanctuary was the earth. Thus as previously shown, it was their faulty interpretation that produced the bitter experience so vividly portrayed in the book of Revelation 10. And Revelation 11:1 has revealed to us that the restoration of knowledge of the sanctuary and its services would not come until the passing of October 22, 1844.

Another necessary point of understanding involves Daniel 8:11–12. The little horn (papal Rome) is clearly portrayed as causing "transgression"[6588] (*pesa*) because he has indeed usurped the prerogatives of God in hearing and presuming to answer prayers, in forgiving sin, and in thinking to change the law of God. With this charge against him, does the little horn then come up for review in the great investigative judgment, or do we look for that process only during the millennium? Turning to the pen of Ellen White, we have these words:

> "As the books of record are opened in the judgment, the lives of all who have believed on Jesus come in review before God. Beginning with those who first lived upon the earth,

our Advocate presents the cases of each successive generation, and closes with the living. Every name is mentioned, every case closely investigated. Names are accepted, names rejected. When any have sins remaining upon the books of record, unrepented of and unforgiven, their names will be blotted out of the book of life, and the record of their good deeds will be erased from the book of God's remembrance." *Great Controversy*, 483.

"At the time appointed for the judgment—the close of the 2300 days, in 1844—began the work of investigation and blotting out of sins. All who have ever taken upon themselves the name of Christ must pass its searching scrutiny. Both the living and the dead are to be judged 'out of those things which were written in the books, according to their works.'" Ibid., 486.

The message is clear. All who have ever taken the name of Christ will be examined thoroughly in the investigative judgment. Does the little horn profess Jesus Christ? Yes, it does. Therefore, the little horn must undergo the investigative judgment, during which his name will either be accepted or rejected. According to Daniel, Paul and John, the little horn is rejected or "cut off," and will also then come under the executive judgment during the 1000-year millennium to receive the reward of her crimes.

As a further point of information in the context of the sanctuary, the time of the end and the judgment, we know of no Seventh-day Adventist that teaches that pagans, heathens and unbelievers (of whom paganism is comprised) are judged this side of the Second Coming. Seventh-day Adventists are united in the belief that the judgment of all those whose unconfessed sins "follow after" (1 Tim 5:24) takes place after the Second Coming, during the 1000-year millennium.

We now come to our third and final noun phrase in Daniel 8:13, "the sanctuary and the host." We will begin with the first of the two nouns in this phrase: "the sanctuary[6944] (*qodes*). Usage: AV - holy 262, sanctuary 68, (holy, hallowed,...) things 52, most 44, holiness 30, dedicated 5, hallowed 3, consecrated 1, misc 3; 382 verses 470 hits.

As we mentioned before, heaven places the sanctuary and the host under one umbrella, "to give *both* . . . to be trodden under foot." The sanctuary that is to be trodden underfoot is a holy sanctuary, the *qodes*. It is none other than the heavenly sanctuary of the new covenant. We now investigate how it is to be trodden underfoot.

"To be trodden[4823] (*mirmas*) under foot." Usage: AV - tread down 4, tread 2, trodden under foot 1; 7 verses 7 hits. "Trodden underfoot" can be a figurative expression, as Paul so clearly illustrates:

> Heb. 10:29 "Of how much sorer punishment, suppose ye, shall he be thought worthy, who hath trodden underfoot the Son of God, and hath counted the blood of the covenant, wherewith he was sanctified, an unholy thing, and hath done despite unto the Spirit of grace?"

As we will show, to defile His name or His sanctuary are synonymous. To defile one is to pollute the other.

> Rev. 13:6 "And he opened his mouth in blasphemy against God, to blaspheme his name, and his tabernacle, and them that dwell in heaven."
> Ps. 74:7 "They have cast fire into thy sanctuary, they have defiled [by casting down] the dwelling place of thy name to the ground."
> Lev. 20:3 "And I will set my face against that man, and will cut him off from among his people; because he hath given of his seed unto Molech, to defile my sanctuary, and to profane my holy name."

Figuratively, then, to have "trodden underfoot" the holy sanctuary and His name is to have trodden underfoot the rightful owner of that sanctuary. In this sense, it is none other than God Almighty. He has obviously been defamed before the entire universe; He's been declared unjust or weak and incompetent.

In ancient Eastern mindset, it was believed that a trampling underfoot of a host or their sanctuary was a trampling underfoot of their god and their religious system. Thus the understanding was that their god was weak and undeserving. Given that connotation of "trodden underfoot," it is understandable why God's government— encompassing, in part, His holy name (character) and law—must be justified and seen in its rightful place of honor.

> "The law of God is the foundation of his Government in Heaven and in earth." *Signs of the Times*, March 30, 1888.

How will this be done? On October 22, 1844, heaven moved into the second apartment of the heavenly sanctuary for the sake of investigation. Christ is eager, through due process and the merits of His blood, to exonerate His people and declare their rightful entry into heaven. Our loving Savior demonstrates to all the unfallen heavenly intelligences that the faithful have indeed washed their robes in the blood of the Lamb. But that is not all that is to be accomplished in the sanctuary during the investigative judgment.

Revelation reveals the primary aspect that cannot be overlooked:

> Rev. 14:7 "Saying with a loud voice, Fear God, and give glory to him; for the hour of his judgment is come: and worship him that made heaven, and earth, and the sea, and the fountains of waters."

Yes, the hour of *His* judgment is come.

God's faithful people living today realize the profound personal relevance of the events taking place in heaven since 1844, but the scriptural emphasis is not exclusively on them. During the cosmic controversy, it is first and foremost God—His character and His government—that has been on trial, with the universe as "courtroom" spectators. It is God's integrity and laws that are being challenged, and His rightful authority to legislate and judge. The Bible says that at the very last remnant of time, just before the Second Coming, God is to be vindicated in a very special way. It is He who will act to sanctify and elevate His holy Law.

"Vindicate" is the last of the three nuances of *sadaq* that is yet to be defined and interpreted. Its place and application in scripture will now be shown.

> Eze. 36:21–3 "But I had pity for mine holy name, which the house of Israel had profaned among the heathen, whither they went. Therefore say unto the house of Israel, Thus saith the Lord GOD; I do not this for your sakes, O house of Israel, but for mine holy name's sake, which ye have profaned among the heathen, whither ye went. And I will sanctify my great name, which was profaned among the heathen, which ye have profaned in the midst of them; and the heathen shall know that I am the LORD, saith the Lord GOD, when I shall be sanctified in you before their eyes."

Again, in the writings of Paul, the Bible is very explicit:

> Rom. 3:4 "God forbid: yea, let God be true, but every man a liar; as it is written, That thou mightest be justified in thy sayings, and mightest overcome when thou art judged."

At the introduction of sin or rebellion in heaven, as depicted in Revelation 12:7–9 and further revealed in *Patriarchs and Prophets*, Lucifer charged the government of heaven—the law of God as well as the Lawgiver, God Himself—with being unjust and unfair. As the following words of Ellen White will reveal, this is the sole reason for the hour of *His* judgment that was and is to come:

> "God could employ only such means as were consistent with truth and righteousness. Satan could use what God could not—flattery and deceit. He had sought to falsify the word of God and had misrepresented His plan of government, claiming that God was not just in imposing laws upon the angels; that in requiring submission and obedience from His creatures, He was seeking merely the exaltation of Himself. It was therefore necessary to demonstrate before the inhabitants of heaven, and of all the worlds, that God's government is just, His law perfect. Satan had made it appear that he himself was seeking to promote the good of the universe. The true character of the usurper and his real object must be understood by all. He must have time to manifest himself by his wicked works." *Patriarchs and Prophets*, 42.

> "He had determined to claim the honor which should have been given [Christ], and take command of all who would become his followers; and he promised those who would enter his ranks a new and better government, under which all would enjoy freedom.

> "God's government included not only the inhabitants of heaven, but of all the worlds that He had created; and Lucifer had concluded that if he could carry the angels of heaven with him in rebellion, he could carry also all the worlds.

> "The discord which his own course had caused in heaven, Satan charged upon the government of God. All evil he declared to be the result of the divine administration. He claimed that it was his own object to improve upon the statutes of Jehovah. Therefore God permitted him to demonstrate the nature of his claims, to show the working out of his proposed changes in the

divine law. His own work must condemn him. Satan had claimed from the first that he was not in rebellion. The whole universe must see the deceiver unmasked.

"Even when he was cast out of heaven, Infinite Wisdom did not destroy Satan. Since only the service of love can be acceptable to God, the allegiance of His creatures must rest upon a conviction of His justice and benevolence. The inhabitants of heaven and of the worlds, being unprepared to comprehend the nature or consequences of sin, could not then have seen the justice of God in the destruction of Satan. Had he been immediately blotted out of existence, some would have served God from fear rather than from love. The influence of the deceiver would not have been fully destroyed, nor would the spirit of rebellion have been utterly eradicated. For the good of the entire universe through ceaseless ages, he must more fully develop his principles, that his charges against the divine government might be seen in their true light by all created beings, and that the justice and mercy of God and the immutability of His law might be forever placed beyond all question.

"Satan's rebellion was to be a lesson to the universe through all coming ages--a perpetual testimony to the nature of sin and its terrible results. The working out of Satan's rule, its effects upon both men and angels, would show what must be the fruit of setting aside the divine authority. It would testify that with the existence of God's government is bound up the well-being of all the creatures He has made. Thus the history of this terrible experiment of rebellion was to be a perpetual safeguard to all holy beings, to prevent them from being deceived as to the nature of transgression, to save them from committing sin, and suffering its penalty." Ibid., 40–42.

The issue is cosmic, to say the least, and the focus of the agitation is vertical, not earthly or horizontal. It is the government of God, the law of God. Today, the Christian world hears the same voice of Satan through his ministers as they promote a so-called new and better government, under a "new" covenant, in which all would enjoy freedom from the bondage of the Law of God. This new covenant of grace, they declare, is confirmed by the writings of Paul in AD 64, found in the book of Colossians 2:14–17, allegedly declaring the law of God to be nailed to the cross. Thus the same warfare as carried out in heaven by Satan and his angels is carried out here on earth by Satan's human instruments.

But thirty-two years after AD 64, we have this testimony of John:

> Rev. 11:19 "And the temple of God was opened in heaven, and there was seen in his temple the ark of his testament."

Moses had been commanded of God to make a sanctuary according to the pattern of the heavenly, so He could dwell among them. Ex. 25:8–9. In that sanctuary was the resting place of the law of God, the ark located in the Most Holy directly under the mercy seat, where God said he would commune with His people. Ex. 25:16, 21–22.

Sixty-five years after the cross, John was given that vision of the heavenly sanctuary. God Himself sits on His throne above the mercy seat, which is situated above the ark of His testament containing the law of God. Thus the very foundation of that throne as seen by John is the ten commandments. They are the written reflection of the nature and character of its Sovereign and the basis of His government of the universe.

> "The cross of Calvary forever condemns the idea that Satan has placed before the Christian world, that the death of Christ abolished not only the typical system of sacrifices and ceremonies but

the unchangeable law of God, the foundation of His throne, the transcript of His character." *Faith and Works*, 90.

This supernatural battle for universal supremacy should be coming clear to the reader as we pull back the veil and reveal why we have been told the hour of His judgment is to, and indeed has, come:

> "In order to endure the trial before them, they must understand the will of God as revealed in His word; they can honor Him only as they have a right conception of His character, government, and purposes, and act in accordance with them." *Great Controversy*, 593.

The government of heaven, as we have seen in this quote, is exhibited in none other than the law of God, a transcript of His character that cannot and does not ever change. Heb. 13:8. It is His purpose that we understand this work of rebellion. The government of Satan must be allowed to be demonstrated before the entire universe, until a time when the entire world unites under a universal bond of Satan's rule. That will be the church's most trying hour. All during the development and culmination of Satan's futile challenge for rulership, we are to act in accordance with the revealed will of God.

Satan's accusations of the brethren and his thrusts that God has been unjust and unfair must and will be met. One can be assured Satan will contest every inch of ground. This scenario will be further played out by the following:

> "In free America, rulers and legislators, in order to secure public favor, will yield to the popular demand for a law enforcing Sunday observance. Liberty of conscience, which has cost so great a sacrifice, will no longer be respected. In the soon–coming conflict we shall see exemplified the prophet's words: 'The dragon was wroth with the

woman, and went to make war with the remnant of her seed, which keep the commandments of God, and have the testimony of Jesus Christ.' Revelation 12:17." *Great Controversy*, 592.

Thus the final crisis will begin, which brings the inhabitants of this world to make a stand with or against the law of God.

> "The so-called Christian world is to be the theater of great and decisive actions. Men in authority will enact laws controlling the conscience, after the example of the papacy. Babylon will make all nations drink of the wine of the wrath of her fornication. Every nation will be involved. Of this time John the Revelator declares:
> "These have one mind.' There will be a universal bond of union, one great harmony, a confederacy of Satan's forces. 'And shall give their power and strength unto the beast.' Thus is manifested the same arbitrary, oppressive power against religious liberty, freedom to worship God according to the dictates of conscience, as was manifested by the papacy, when in the past it persecuted those who dared to refuse to conform to the religious rites and ceremonies of Romanists.
> "In the warfare to be waged in the last days there will be united, in opposition to God's people, all the corrupt powers that have apostatized from allegiance to the law of Jehovah. In this warfare the Sabbath of the fourth commandment will be the great point at issue, for in the Sabbath commandment the great Lawgiver identifies Himself as the Creator of the heavens and the earth." *Selected Messages*, 3:392–3.

Yet God is at last to be vindicated, and the government of heaven will never again be contested throughout the ceaseless ages.

"Satan is constantly at work, with intense energy and under a thousand disguises, to misrepresent the character and government of God. With extensive, well-organized plans and marvelous power, he is working to hold the inhabitants of the world under his deceptions. God, the One infinite and all-wise, sees the end from the beginning, and in dealing with evil His plans were far-reaching and comprehensive. It was His purpose, not merely to put down the rebellion, but to demonstrate to all the universe the nature of the rebellion. God's plan was unfolding, showing both His justice and His mercy, and *fully vindicating* His wisdom and righteousness in His dealings with evil By the facts unfolded in the progress of the great controversy, God will demonstrate the principles of His rules of government, which have been falsified by Satan and by all whom he has deceived. His justice will finally be acknowledged by the whole world, though the acknowledgment will be made too late to save the rebellious. God carries with Him the sympathy and approval of the whole universe as step by step His great plan advances to its complete fulfillment. He will carry it with Him in the final eradication of rebellion. It will be seen that all who have forsaken the divine precepts have placed themselves on the side of Satan, in warfare against Christ. When the prince of this world shall be judged, and all who have united with him shall share his fate, the whole universe as witnesses to the sentence will declare, 'Just and true are Thy ways, Thou King of saints.' Revelation 15:3." *Patriarchs and Prophets*, 78–9, emphasis added.

"The warfare against God's law, which was begun in heaven, will be continued until the end of time. Every man will be tested. Obedience or disobedience is the question to be decided by the whole world. All will be called to choose between the law of God and the laws of men. Here the dividing line will be drawn. There will be but two classes. Every character will be fully developed; and all will show whether they have chosen the side of loyalty or that of rebellion. Then the end will come. *God will vindicate His law* and deliver His people." *Desire of Ages*, 763, emphasis added.

"The final judgment is a most solemn, awful event. This must take place before the universe. To the Lord Jesus the Father has committed all judgment. He will declare the reward of loyalty to the law of Jehovah. God will be honored and *His government vindicated and glorified*, and that in the presence of the inhabitants of the unfallen worlds. *On the largest possible scale will the government of God be vindicated and exalted.* It is not the judgment of one individual or of one nation, but *of the whole world*. Oh, what a change will then be made in the understanding of all created beings. Then all will see the value of eternal life."–Letter 131, Oct. 14, 1900, to Elder A. G. Daniells; *Manuscript Releases*, 21:349, emphasis added.

Even after the close of probation, the scriptures yet portray the vindication of God by His people along with the unfallen agencies of heaven.

Rev. 15:4 "Who shall not fear Thee and glorify Thy name, for Thou only art holy"[3741] (*hosios*).

The Greek word for "holy" is not the one commonly interpreted so. This particular word *hosios* denotes that which is "right," and it involves the vindication of God, especially in His pronouncement of a righteous and just verdict. It is a recognition of moral obligations.

Gen. 18:25 "Shall not the judge of all the earth do right?"

When God metes out His judgments in the seven last plagues, it will be a revelation of His righteousness and justice in the great controversy between Christ and Satan, in which the remnant have played a significant part. In both the investigative and executive judgments, He shows Himself to be and is declared to be just.

The unfallen creation are also represented as recognizing the rightful judgments of the Creator:

> Rev. 16:5-7 "And I heard the angel of the waters say, Thou art righteous, O Lord, which art, and wast, and shalt be, because thou hast judged thus. For they have shed the blood of saints and prophets, and thou hast given them blood to drink; for they are worthy. And I heard another out of the altar say, Even so, Lord God Almighty, true and righteous are thy judgments."

Before the universe, the remnant will proclaim the righteousness and justice of God's dealings. On earth, under the severest test, they will have displayed their loyalty and obedience. They will have proved that God's law can be kept even under the most dire circumstances. God will then be cleared of all accusations before the universe.

> Ps. 51:4 "That thou mightest be justified when thou speakest, and be clear when thou judgest."

Therefore, when the heavenly sanctuary of Daniel 8:13, which has been "trodden underfoot" for centuries by the false accusations leveled against the God of that sanctuary, is "cleansed" (*nitsdaq*), it will be manifest before all that its God will most surely be "vindicated" (*sadaq*) in the hour of His judgment. This interpretation bears the test of investigation.

We now begin our consideration of "the host"[6635] (*saba*). "Host" is the second noun in the third noun phrase of Daniel 8:13, and the concluding topic of our study of verses thirteen and fourteen in Daniel 8. Usage: AV - host 393, war 41, army 29, battle 5, service 5, appointed time

3, warfare 2, soldiers 1, company 1, misc 5; 461 verses 485 hits. In the context of Daniel 8:13, the host is clearly the people of God, and the trampling underfoot of the host refers to none other than the persecution of the saints.

In Daniel 8:10, 12, 24, as well as Daniel 7:25, we witnessed a very specific time period during which the saints were to be trodden underfoot: when the papacy was permitted to "practice and prosper" for 1260 long years.

As shown, this prophesied trampling of the host would occur prior to 1844. It is in Daniel 12:7 that the portion of Daniel's question regarding the treading underfoot of the host is answered, showing that the trampling and scattering of the saints would be until 1798:

> Dan. 12:7 "And I heard the man clothed in linen, which was upon the waters of the river, when he held up his right hand and his left hand unto heaven, and sware by him that liveth for ever that it shall be for a time, times, and an half; and when he shall have accomplished to scatter the power of the holy people, all these things shall be finished."

During the Dark Ages of papal rule, when over fifty million of God's people were condemned to death for their faith and loyalty to Christ, they were judged and presented in the most dark and malicious light before the world. The events culminating in October 22, 1844, and the renewed understanding of heaven's sanctuary, prove that depiction false beyond doubt. In that understanding, God again demonstrates His faithfulness to His moral obligations. When the investigative judgment concludes, God's Word reveals the saints in their true light, picturing them in garments of purest white, with a righteous judgment given in favor of the saints. God is vindicated, as well as the faithful of all ages. Rev. 19:8; Dan. 7:22. The "restoration," "cleansing," and "vindication" (*sadaq* meanings) foretold in the sanctuary's cleansing (*nitsdaq*, with all of the nuances of *sadaq* implied for Daniel 8:13), is finally and forever accomplished.

# 9

# DANIELLS AND PRESCOTT ISSUES

So far in our studies, we have been able to penetrate the scriptures and historical sources to a fuller and deeper extent than heretofore possible. Everyone is now equipped to explain the prophetic implications of the relevant events of AD 508 and 538 which began the 1260- and 1290-year time prophecies of Daniel 8. The pivotal issues of church and state, as well as the law of God, have been clearly defined in our study. Correctly interpreted, the "daily" can now be understood in its full sanctuary significance. And by itself, the "transgression of desolation," rightly comprehended, can be seen in its unique role in our sanctuary message; a misinterpretation of "transgression of desolation" has been shown to have removed the investigative judgment from Daniel 8.

When believers must stand alone to answer for their faith, what reproach to the cause of truth—and what disillusionment and even grief to its holders—if they would learn too late they have had no Biblical foundation for their beliefs, and that perhaps they had been misrepresenting the truth all along. Hence, the sole purpose of this book has been to bring to the fore the truth on the "daily" and its related issues.

The correct scriptural and historical understanding of the "daily" has vindicated the very nucleus of our sanctuary message and has fortified the reader with the necessary documentation to rightfully answer "every man that asketh you a reason of the hope that is in you with meekness and fear." 1 Peter 3:15.

As we near the close of this study, we will expand upon some significant points already discussed and deal with some misconceptions that have not been previously addressed. We want to be thorough and complete in our study, so we can once and for all lay this issue to rest.

Our attention will first center on an error of understanding that would silence any discussion of the "daily" and discourage any consideration that the "daily" issue can and was to be resolved. A few passages from an undated work have been erroneously cited to prove a false premise. The passages come from *Manuscript Releases* (MR), Volume 20, pages 17–22, also called *Manuscript Release No. 1425* and entitled "Errors and Dangers of Prescott and Daniells; The Cities to Be Worked." It is obvious from the title and context that the manuscript was written during the General Conference presidency of A. G. Daniells. This manuscript was at one time mistakenly given a later date than *Manuscript Release No. 1470*, which may confuse researchers. In truth, though, *Manuscript Release No. 1425* has neither day nor month nor year dating it. This mistake in dating has been corrected, and Tim Poirier of the Ellen G. White Estate of the General Conference of Seventh-day Adventists can confirm these facts.

The false premise is that to accept the "daily" as the work of the priest in the first apartment is to be "worked by the angels that were expelled from heaven," as Daniells and Prescott admittedly were at the time of her writing, and to incorporate sentiments of a spiritualistic nature, which would bring in unbelief and skepticism. For those reasons, it is claimed, Ellen White completely condemned the ministry view of the "daily."

The unlikely premise Mrs. White's manuscript is said to support, as per the brief excerpt quoted in the previous paragraph, is handily disproved for all to see by the following study. Before exposing the error, however, we will also quote a specific longer passage from the same manuscript that is additionally used to support claims against the true interpretation of the "daily." Ellen White wrote:

> "I was shown that Brother Daniells and Brother Prescott were weaving into their experience sentiments of a spiritualistic appearance and drawing our people to beautiful sentiments

that would deceive, if possible, the very elect. I have to trace with my pen [the fact] that these brethren would see defects in their delusive ideas that would place the truth in an uncertainty; and [yet] they [would] stand out as [if they had] great spiritual discernment. Now I am to tell them [that] when I was shown this matter, when Elder Daniells was lifting up his voice like a trumpet in advocating his ideas of the "Daily," the after results were presented. Our people were becoming confused. I saw the result, and then there were given me cautions that if Elder Daniells without respect to the outcome should thus be impressed and let himself believe he was under the inspiration of God, skepticism would be sown among our ranks everywhere, and we should be where Satan would carry his messages. Set unbelief and skepticism would be sown in human minds, and strange crops of evil would take the place of truth." *Manuscript Releases*, 20:17, 18, 21–22.

Admittedly, taken out of its context, this passage and the manuscript's earlier reference to demonic influence look quite straightforward and rather incriminating. Before commenting, though, we want to encourage all to read the entire manuscript for themselves. Remember, brothers and sisters, assume nothing and require proof of all things.

Let us now read these quotes in a fuller context, in order to derive the true and intended meaning of the passage. We will begin at the beginning of the manuscript and will quote enough to give content in honest context. Bracketing is in the original.

"At this stage of our experience we are not to have our minds drawn away from the special light given [us] to consider at the important gathering of our conference. And there was Brother Daniells, whose mind the enemy was working; and your mind and Elder Prescott's mind were being worked by the angels that were expelled from heaven. Satan's work was to divert your minds that jots and tittles should be brought in which the Lord did not inspire you to bring in. They were not essential. But this meant much to the cause of truth. And the ideas of your minds, if you could be drawn away to jots or tittles, is a work of Satan's devising. To correct little things in the books written, you suppose would be doing a great work. But I am charged, Silence is eloquence.

"I am to say, Stop your picking flaws. If this purpose of the devil could only be carried out, then [it] appears to you [that] your work would be considered as most wonderful in conception. It was the enemy's plan to get all the supposed objectionable features where all classes of minds did not agree. And what then? The very work that pleases the devil would come to pass. There would be a representation given to the outsiders not of our faith just what would suit them, that would develop traits of character which would cause great confusion and occupy the golden moments which should be used zealously to bring the great message before the people. The presentations upon any subject we have worked upon could not all harmonize, and the results would be to confuse the minds of believers and unbelievers. This is the very thing that Satan had planned that should take place--anything that could be magnified as a disagreement.

"Read Ezekiel, chapter 28. Now, here is a grand work, where strange spirits can figure. But the Lord has a work to [be] done to save perishing souls."

"And I was shown from the first that the Lord had given neither Elders Daniells nor Prescott the burden of this work. Should Satan's wiles be brought in, should this "Daily" be such a great matter as to be brought in to confuse minds and hinder the advancement of the work at this important period of time? It should not, whatever may be. This subject should not be introduced. There would be confusion brought into our ranks. You have no call to hunt up the difference of opinion that is not a testing question; but your silence is eloquence. Now the work without delay is to be taken up and not a [difference] of opinion expressed."

"I was instructed to say to you that your picking flaws in the writings of men that have been led of God is not inspired of God."

"Now, everything like picking flaws in the publications of men who are not alive is not the work God has given any of you to do. For if these men had followed the directions given in working the cities."

"But let us now investigate the matter. We must now reconsider whether it is the Lord's judgment, in the face of the work that has been neglected, of showing your zeal to carry the work even another year." (Addressed to Daniells.–ed.)

"The Lord will have to see in you a showing of a different experience, for if ever men needed to be reconverted at this present [time], it [is] Elder Daniells and Elder Prescott.

"The crisis has come, for God will be dishonored.

"How does the Lord look upon the unworked cities?" *Manuscript Releases*, 20:17–20.

Brothers and sisters, we again encourage you to read Ellen White's entire manuscript for yourselves. Regarding the "daily," is it not plain at this point in the manuscript that Daniells and Prescott were being severely reproved for debating the lesser issue of the "daily" at the expense of a far more important work they'd earlier been counseled to undertake? We find no discussion of the actual interpretation of the "daily" thus far. Only indirect references were made to the "daily," and none had to do with interpretation.

And is it not evident they also were taking upon themselves the critiquing the writings of earlier stalwarts of the Advent faith, thus bringing needless confusion among believers and exposing the dear cause to public scorn? Ellen White gave forceful directives to Brothers Daniells and Prescott to leave the books of the Advent faith alone. (Elder Prescott in particular wanted to correct what he perceived to be historical inaccuracies in some of Mrs. White's published works.) Their actions were met with strong reproof because rather than obeying the call to work the cities, they were weakening and confusing the young church by discrediting the work of faithful men who, although mistaken in some of their positions, nevertheless poured heart and soul and means into the early years of the new prophetic understandings. Furthermore, Ellen White disapproved of the methods they were using.

> "Where was your respect for the men of age? What authority could you exercise without taking all the responsible men to weigh the matter?" *Manuscript Releases*, 20:19.

No wonder Ellen White called into question Daniells' role as conference president.

Having found neither support nor disapproval of Daniells' view of the "daily" so far in the manuscript, let us continue to see if such a reference can truly be found.

> "What would you gain if mistakes are brought before the men who have departed from the faith and given heed to seducing spirits, men who were not long ago with us in the faith? Will you stand on the devil's side? Give your attention to the unworked fields. A world-wide work is before us. I was given representations of John Kellogg. A very attractive personage was representing the ideas of the specious arguments

that he was presenting, sentiments different from the genuine Bible truth. And those who are hungering and thirsting after something new were advancing ideas [so specious] that Elder Prescott was in great danger. Elder Daniells was in great danger [of] becoming wrapped in a delusion that if these sentiments could be spoken everywhere it would be as a new world.

"Yes, it would, but while their minds were thus absorbed I was shown that Brother Daniells and Brother Prescott were weaving into their experience sentiments of a spiritualistic appearance and drawing our people to beautiful sentiments that would deceive, if possible, the very elect. I have to trace with my pen [the fact] that these brethren would see defects in their delusive ideas that would place the truth in an uncertainty; and [yet] they [would] stand out as [if they had] great spiritual discernment. Now I am to tell them [that] when I was shown this matter, when Elder Daniells was lifting up his voice like a trumpet in advocating his ideas of the 'Daily,' the after results were presented. Our people were becoming confused. I saw the result, and then there were given me cautions that if Elder Daniells without respect to the outcome should thus be impressed and let himself believe he was under the inspiration of God, skepticism would be sown among our ranks everywhere, and we should be where Satan would carry his messages. Set unbelief and skepticism would be sown in human minds, and strange crops of evil would take the place of truth." *Manuscript Releases*, 20:21-22, bracketing in original.

Let us remember that at the turn of the twentieth century, this first decade under the conference presidential reign of Elder Daniells was one of utmost chaos, to say the least. Among the causes of the confusion, embarrassment and distress were the wide circulation of

D. M. Canright's book *Seventh Day Adventism Renounced*, the fires of the Battle Creek Sanitarium and the Review and Herald publishing house, the apostasy of prominent Brothers A. T. Jones and E. J. Waggoner, and the public disputes about the writings of Ellen White, both within and without the church. The church also had to confront the damage caused by the apostasy of A. F. Ballenger, the diminishment or denial of the sanctuary message so lately understood, and the spiritualistic sentiments expressed in pantheism and espoused by the influential J. H. Kellogg.

Hence the counsel was given to do the work of the Lord, meaning to work the cities for the saving of souls, and to bring nothing to the front, including the topic of the "daily," that would foster strife and division among the early believers, and elicit scorn and derision from the enemies of the faith. And as can now be seen by all, the "sentiments of a spiritualistic appearance" that Ellen White noted in that manuscript do not refer to the "daily" at all. In fact, they plainly relate to the spiritualistic influences of pantheism advocated by J. H. Kellogg that Daniells and Prescott were "weaving" about themselves and others.

Over and over again, the reproval in Ellen White's letters centered on Daniells' neglect of heeding the counsel to work the cities for the saving of souls. Instead, he was trying to use his position as General Conference president to settle doctrinal controversy over the "daily." This battle of interpretations had engendered a very "forbidding spirit" on both sides of the issue, thus bringing in additional confusion and dismay. Thus we see that Daniells' need to be "reconverted" stemmed largely from his neglect to heed God's counsel to work the cities, not his advocacy of the "ministry of Christ" view of the "daily."

In confirmation of that fact, we now include, in part, a six-page article that Arthur L. White wrote on December 4, 1953—an article appropriately called *Concerning Elder A. G. Daniells*. In this document Arthur White demonstrated the true nature of events that took place:

"That there was a crisis in 1910 involving Elder A. G. Daniells, none can deny. He spoke of it publicly, and we quote his words as taken from one of a series of talks he gave on the Spirit of prophecy to a group of workers in Australia in 1928:

"'Sister White gave me counsel and reproof concerning many matters. She sent messages to me regarding the work in the cities in the Eastern States. I seemed unable to understand them fully. Consequently I did not do all that these messages indicated should be done. Finally I received a message in which she said, "When the president of the General Conference is converted, he will know what to do with the messages God has sent him." I did not then have as much light on the matter of conversion as I now have. I thought I had been converted fifty years before, and so I had; but I have since learned that we need to be reconverted now and then. We need a fresh, up-to-date experience in repentance and conversion frequently, so that we shall be able to receive fresh light and grace and understanding for the problems that are continually arising. That message, telling me that I needed to be converted, cut me severely at the time, but I did not reject it. I began to pray for the conversion I needed to give me the understanding I seemed to lack.

"'The pressure regarding work for the great cities became so great that I finally arranged the work of the General Conference with my associates, and went with my wife to New York City, to stay just as long as it was my duty. When I had been there a few weeks, a new vision came to me regarding the needs of our great cities. I wrote my impressions to Sister White; I thanked her for her reproof and instruction. I told her that I was quite ready to resign my office and devote myself to the millions in these great cities, and asked for further counsel. She wrote back a good motherly letter, expressing great gratitude for the light that had come to me, and telling me that it was not for me to resign, but to use all the influence of my position to forward that work and to draw others into those great cities.' --<u>Australasian</u> <u>Union</u> <u>Conference</u> <u>Record</u>, August 13, 1928.

"Elder Daniells made no reference in this statement to the question of the health message or the 'daily' of Daniel 8. Going back to the General Conference of 1909, we find that Ellen White was much concerned for the spiritual experience of the leading workers. She was eager that they should lead out in the important lines of work which should have first attention, and she presented a number of cautions and appeals which were directed to the president of the General Conference and his close associates.

"For half a decade prior to 1910 there was some agitation in the denomination concerning the 'daily' of Daniel 8. Both those who stood by the views presented by Elder Uriah Smith in Thoughts on Daniel and the Revelation and those who saw light in an interpretation which differed, were very earnest in their declarations. The matter was one which could have been settled by open minded study, or relegated to a subordinate place, but it attracted such attention that it diverted minds from the important work of proclaiming the message of warning to a perishing world. (Pg. 1.)

"During this time Ellen White was pleading for the large cities of America, as it seemed to be the opportune time to make great advances in that particular line. But with the president of the General Conference, Elder Daniells, and some of his associates carrying the burden of the world work, and now with the added burden of the discussions on the 'daily' of Daniel 8, the advance steps called for in city work in America

were not taken. In no uncertain terms Elder Daniells and his associates were reproved for this neglect and for giving undue attention to matters of minor importance. Elder Daniells' response to the reproof and instruction was whole hearted, a response translated into action which was fully accepted of the Lord.
"While the details of the story which we shall present show the marked influence of the Spirit of prophecy in the movement, and also the greatness of a man who altered his course to walk in the light, there would be no occasion to make the matter public were it not for the distribution of the reports which have been sent out to our workers which disparages Elder Daniells."

The reason there had been "some agitation concerning the 'daily' of Daniel 8" for "half a decade prior to 1910" is revealed in the following portion of the same Arthur White article regarding the denominational crisis engendered by General Conference President A. G. Daniells' failure to heed the counsel to work the cities:

### "What Actually Took Place

"On May 24, 1910, Mrs. E. G. White called Elder W. C. White to her room and asked what was being done in regard to the teaching of the new and old views of the 'daily.' She asked why those who were leading out in these discussions did not get together and study the matter unitedly, and she expressed regret that such a meeting had not been held. On that same day she dispatched a letter to Elder S. N. Haskell, and directed that copies should be sent to Elders Loughborough, Irwin, and Daniells. In this she made an appeal for the brethren who were then on the Pacific Coast, including those named above and also Elder Salisbury to come together in 'examination of the points of faith regarding which there are different views.' The meeting failed to materialize." (Pg. 2.)

Mrs. White's concerns about the intradenominational confusion and controversy arising from the publication of "different views" of the "daily" resulted in her written appeal that the gentlemen "come together" to resolve the matter. Because of the spiritualistic influence attributed to Daniells and the misleading quotation of Ellen White from *Manuscript Releases 1425*, as exposed and rectified earlier in this chapter, we think it best to include the original of that manuscript addressed to the elders. Mrs. White's own words will prove beyond doubt that to advocate that Ellen White likened Elder Daniells' ministry interpretation of the "daily" to spiritualistic sentiments, and to charge Daniells with having been so unconverted as to bring in unbelief and skepticism via spiritualism, is to shortchange believers and negatively affect understanding in two respects.

First of all, the following letter will show that if those charges were true, then Ellen White promoted and demanded the study of spiritualistic sentiments that bear the fruit of unbelief and skepticism. There is no escape from this conclusion, as we shall see.

> MR No. 1470 - Doctrines to Be Investigated; Unity to Be Sought (Written May 24, 1910, from Sanitarium, California, to Elder and Mrs. S. N. Haskell.)
> "I have been waiting for the time when there should be an investigation of the doctrines that Brother Daniells and others have been advocating. When is this to be?
> "If Elder Daniells thinks that some of the interpretations of Scripture that have been held in the past are not correct, our brethren should listen to his reasons, and give candid consideration to his views. All should examine closely their own standing, and by a thorough

knowledge of the principles of our faith, be prepared to vindicate the truth.

"We must not be inconsistent in this matter. God requires clean hearts, pure minds, and an intelligent belief in the truth. 'Faith is the substance of things hoped for, the evidence of things not seen.' At present there is not that unity that should exist among our brethren, and the Lord says, 'Come together.' This should be done as soon as possible, for we have no time to lose.

"Is not the present a favorable time for you and others of our ministering brethren in this conference to meet with Elder Daniells for a thorough examination of the points of faith regarding which there are different views?

"[Isaiah 11:1-16; 12:1-6, quoted.]

"I am directed to write these Scriptures for the consideration of those who shall assemble for the purpose of blending together under the guidance of the Holy Spirit. 'Bind up the testimony, seal the law among My disciples.' A special work now rests upon us of solemnly investigating these matters, and in the name of the Lord to unify." Letter 50, 1910; *Manuscript Releases*, 20:223.

The fact that Ellen White put the burden of proof on Elders Haskell, Loughborough and others to consider Elder Daniells' ministry position on the "daily" lends itself to no other conclusion but that the accusations against Daniells are totally untenable and are a misrepresentation of Ellen White's writings. Furthermore, Ellen White, in encouraging the comparative study of all interpretations of the "daily" to determine its correct meaning, cannot be said to have wittingly or unwittingly supported in any way any so–called spiritualistic positions held by Daniells. To so believe would be to challenge and undermine the credibility of God's prophet.

Secondly, there has been further misuse of Ellen White's writings by those who state that she condemned the "ministry of Christ" view held by Elder Daniells. We trust it is not their intention, but they have now made her into a liar and a false prophet. How can the prophet condemn Elder Daniels when he himself but advocated the very expressed understandings of Ellen White published in 1890:

> "As Christ's ministration was to consist of two great divisions, each occupying a period of time and having a distinctive place in the heavenly sanctuary, so the typical ministration consisted of two divisions, the *daily* and the yearly service, and to each a department of the tabernacle was devoted. As Christ at His ascension appeared in the presence of God to plead His blood in behalf of penitent believers, so the priest in the *daily ministration* sprinkled the blood of the sacrifice in the holy place in the sinner's behalf." *Patriarchs and Prophets*, 357, emphasis added.

Also, some twenty-two years before her written directive to settle the matter of the "daily," she'd also written:

> "The ministration of the earthly sanctuary consisted of two divisions; the priests ministered *daily* in the holy place, while once a year the high priest performed a special work of atonement in the most holy, for the cleansing of the sanctuary. *Day by day* the repentant sinner brought his offering to the door of the tabernacle [first apartment] and, placing his hand upon the victim's head, confessed his sins, thus in figure transferring them from himself to the innocent sacrifice. Such was the work that went on, *day by day*, throughout the year. The sins of Israel were thus transferred to the sanctuary, and a special work became necessary for their removal." *Great Controversy* (1888), 442; (1911), 418, emphasis supplied.

Thus this aspect of our "daily" study closes with charges of spiritualism against Daniells explained, and other misrepresentations from *Manuscript 1425* presented in honest context.

Readers may be wondering what ultimately happened to Elder Daniells regarding his General Conference presidency and whether his relationship with Ellen White was ever restored. While it is true that Ellen White would not see or talk to Elder Daniells at or around the time of his ignoring of her counsel, the ice was finally broken after Elder Daniells penitently heeded the counsel. We gladly relay that Elder Daniells wrote once more in the context of this topic, this time from New York City while engaged in his evangelistic effort for the salvation of souls with the Advent message. Brother Arthur L. White's report will fill in this part of exciting history, and certainly will reveal the loving and forgiving God we serve.

> "On July 1 Elder Daniells presented to the General Conference Committee the communications he had received from Sister White, and it was decided that the city work should have first attention. A committee of seventeen was appointed to oversee this work. Elder Daniells was released from campmeeting appointments and a trip to Australia, and his administrative responsibilities were delegated to two or three of the officers in Washington, allowing him to go to New York City to personally conduct an evangelistic effort.
>
> "In the days that followed he pondered the full significance of the suggestion made by Sister white that, if he failed to walk in the way God would have him go, it would be well if he laid aside his responsibilities as president of the General Conference. On August 5 he wrote to Elder W. C. White, with the understanding that his communication would be placed before Sister White, pointing out that he was not certain just what course of action he should follow, but, under

the counsel and advice of his brethren, he had reached the conclusion that he should go forward in leading out in the work in the cities, and should not make an immediate decision as to the future of his administrative work. He then declared:

"'Now Brother White, I am doing the very best I know how to follow the instruction in the Testimonies and to be true to this cause. That is all I can say. There is a world of work to be done in other lands which is very inviting to me, and all I ask is that I may be allowed to quietly arrange the changes that will be necessary when it is time for me to go.'

"This letter was read by Sister White on August 11, and on the same day Elder White wrote to Elder Daniells as follows:

"'This morning Mother read your letter of August 5, written by yourself early in the morning. It took her a long time to read it because she stopped every two or three paragraphs to make comments. How I wished I were a stenographer and could write it down and give it to you just as she talked. Mother told me that she thought you were taking just the right course, and that she believed the Lord would greatly bless you in giving yourself personally to the evangelistic work. She said that in the night in her dreams she was talking to you and telling you that it was not best for you now to resign your place as President of the General Conference, but that you were to use all your tact and experience and all the influence that your position gives you in helping, strengthening, and building up the evangelistic work, and that you were to encourage your brother ministers who have been devoting their time to business affairs, to follow your example in putting the business responsibility upon others and entering personally into labor and into a study of the work to be done by our preachers for the masses.

"'When Mother was done telling me about this, she requested me to write to you. I told her I would do so, but I hoped that she would write the matter for herself, for while you would receive my words and give credit to my statements, there were others who would greatly prefer to Pg. 3. have her own statement of the matter over her signature. About noon Mother brought over a two-page letter that she has written which will be copied and go forward to you tomorrow, I think.'"—W. C. White to A. G. Daniells, August 11, 1910.

"Reference was made in the communication quoted above to a letter written by Sister White, in which she indicates a full acceptance of the change in the experience of Elder A. G. Daniells, and her confidence in him as president of the General Conference. Her communication in its entirety follows:

"'Sanitarium, Calif.           "'Aug. 11, 1910
"'Elder A. G. Daniells:
"'Dear Brother, --

"'I have received your letters regarding the council held in New York, and the efforts that are being made in behalf of the multitudes in the large cities. I have also read your letters of August 4 and 5 to W. C. White. I intended to answer your letters immediately, but I have been carrying so heavy a burden that I thought I must wait till I could write you clearly.
"'The position you have taken is in the order of the Lord, and now I would encourage you with the words, Go forward as you have begun, using your position of influence as President of the General Conference for the advancement of the work we are called upon to do. In this way you can disappoint the enemy. You will need all the influence that the Lord gives you as a wise leader

to encourage your associates in responsibility to take hold of the city work, and carry it forward in a sensible way.

"'I am glad for this letter you have sent me, telling us of what you are doing. The light that I have from the Lord is that this same experience will be needed by others. You will now be able, not only to take up the work yourself, but also to exercise your influence as president of the General Conference to lead out in the very work that the Lord has appointed to be done.

"'You cannot be spared now from the work that has been so long left undone. The Lord has given you an opportunity to redeem the time, and cover the neglect of the past. I can now take hold with you in full confidence for the doing of the work that rests upon us. The Lord in His mercy will pardon the failure of the past. He will be your helper. He will give you sustaining grace, and we will draw with you and give you all the help we can to use your position of influence as president of the Conference, and to work wisely in the education of others to labor in the cities.

"'Your influence will be under the Lord's wise care, and although you may meet hard and trying experiences in this great effort, if you exercise the wisdom and the sanctification of Christ, you will have power and grace from above, and the Lord's approval. He will impart unto you wisdom and power, and will also bring to you the joy of success.

Pg. 4.

"'I am so thankful that you have written us how you have given yourself to this work. Angels of God will be with you, and you can use all the influence that your office as president of the Conference has given you, to encourage others to take up the same work. I will not write a word to discourage you or to weaken your hands, but will say, Go forward in the name of the Lord. His name is a power against the enemy.

"'I have had several days of illness. It seems as though Satan would take my life. I am weak, but not discouraged. Several nights it has seemed that I could not live till morning, but I am now venturing to write this, lest the enemy shall discourage you.

"'In conclusion I will say, Redeem the lost time of the past nine years by going ahead now with the work in our cities, and the Lord will bless and sustain you.' –E. G. White, Letter 68, 1910.

"It is therefore clear, that, while for a time in 1910 Elder Daniells was not standing in the full light when the messages of reproof and rebuke were sent to him, he heeded the counsel. This placed him in an entirely different light in the eyes of the Lord.

## "Mrs. White's Confidence in Elder Daniells and Other Leaders

"Mrs. White's confidence in Elder Daniells was maintained through the rest of her life. In 1912, when she was drawing up her will and was making provision for a Board of Trustees who should carry the responsibility of the custody of her writings after her death, she named five men, and among these was Elder A. G. Daniells. In no more forceful way could she indicate her confidence in a man than by naming him to this important work.

"In 1913 the General Conference Session was again held in Washington, D. C. It was not possible for Sister White to be present, so she addressed two communications to be read to the delegates. In the first of these she made reference to the 1909 session, and expressed her apprehension over the course of events if there had not been a change in the attitude of certain men. She then acknowledged her recognition of the change which took place, and expressed confidence in her brethren who were carrying the burdens of responsibility. We give here a portion of this communication which was read to the delegates in session, for it expresses Ellen White's attitude to the leadership of the movement at that late date:

"'During the General Conference of 1909, a work should have been done in the hearts of those in attendance that was not done. Hours should have been given up to heart-searching, that would have led to the breaking up of the fallow ground of the hearts of those who were at the meeting. This would have given them insight to understand the work so essential to be done by them in repentance and confession. But, though opportunities were given for confession of sin, for heart-felt repentance, and for a decided reformation, thorough work was not done. Some felt the influence of the Holy Spirit, and responded; but all did not yield to this influence. The minds of some were running in forbidden channels. Had there been on the part of all in the assembly a humbling of heart, there would have been manifested a wonderful blessing.

Pg. 5.

"'For a number of months after the close of that meeting, I bore a heavy burden, and urged upon the attention of the brethren in responsibility those things which the Lord was instructing me to set before them plainly. <u>Finally some of those in positions of trust in connection with the general work, after much prayer and careful study of the various messages given, ventured to undertake by faith the work called for, --a work they could not fully understand; and as they went forward in the fear of God, they received rich blessing.</u>

"'It has brought great rejoicing to my heart to see the marvelous transformations that have been

wrought in the lives of some who thus chose to advance by faith in the way of the Lord, rather than to follow a way of their own choosing. <u>Had those brethren in responsibility continued to view matters in a false light, they would have created a condition of things that would badly have marred the work; but when they heeded the instruction that was sent, and sought the Lord, God brought them into the full light, and enabled them to render acceptable service and to bring about spiritual reformations.</u>
"'When the Lord sets His hand to prepare the way before His ministers, it is their duty to follow where He directs. He will never forsake or leave in uncertainty those who follow His leadings with full purpose of heart. 'I rejoice,' my brethren, 'that I have confidence in you in all things.' --E. G. White in <u>The General Conference Bulletin</u>, May 19, 1913, p. 34. [Emphasis Arthur White's.]
Arthur L. White
Ellen G. White Publications
General Conference
December 4, 1953
Pg. 6."

With the facts clearly presented before all, none need be troubled by the inappropriate use of *Manuscript Releases No. 1425* again. It is of a truth that Ellen White received no light on the "daily" from the vision of 1850 related in *Early Writings*, pg. 74–5. But it would be false to say that Ellen White never since that time received light and understanding as to what the "daily" is. This fact has been demonstrated and forcefully illustrated. In the most candid and straightforward manner, she leaves no one in doubt as to her position and understanding in this matter. She wrote of Christ's daily and yearly service in the heavenly sanctuary. But never does she say the "daily" is paganism.

# 10

## THE SANCTUARY IS THE LORD'S

We declared that the sanctuary of Daniel 8:11 was the heavenly sanctuary, and we said we would further confirm that fact. It is here that we will revisit this issue of the sanctuary and illustrate its connection to the Hebrew word *chazon* (vision), thus showing conclusively, again from the scriptures, that the sanctuary in Daniel 8:11, 13, 14 is none other than the heavenly sanctuary. We will begin by addressing some lingering points of controversy not previously mentioned in the context of the "daily."

First, in the past and even today, some church members believe, and some even teach, that many leaders of the early church left the faith because they accepted and were misled by the view of the "daily" as being the ministry of Christ. A long list of names of men who supposedly abandoned their advent beliefs is cited to support this understanding.

Once again, brothers and sisters, nothing could be further from the truth. No documentation has been produced for this claim because there is none. A mere listing of names certainly provides no evidence as to the true reason those listed left, nor has that evidence ever been published. Actually, many of the men named on the list echoed the same sentiments found in *Patriarchs and Prophets*, 357, and *Great Controversy*, 418. They were not adherents of the paganism view.

Frankly, the charge of leaving the faith because of acceptance of erroneous interpretation actually can be said of someone holding the paganism view. And, indeed, there does exist documentation that proves specifically that acceptance of the paganism view caused a man to leave the faith because of its many gross inconsistencies. The evidence is in the following letter.

E. J. Hibbard, writing to Elder L. A. Smith (son of Uriah Smith) in Nashville, Tennessee, from San Fernando, California, on October 24, 1909, was at one time an advocate of the paganism view himself. He later changed his view because of the several incongruities he discovered, and humbly admitted his mistake. In this letter, Hibbard attempted to help Smith see the shaky foundation of paganism that Smith was trying to build upon. Just one year after Uriah Smith's book on Daniel came out, Hibbard related to Smith how he himself had begun to see and understand the truth:

> "Dear Brother: Elder L. A. Smith,
> "As I have a little time this morning, I will endeavor to reply more fully to the questions contained in your letter of the 17th inst.
> "In the spring, of 1874 while holding quarterly meeting in Bear Lake, Penn., elder L. A. Wing, who had been led to give up all three of the messages on account of the inconsistency of the old position on 'the daily', invited me to read Dan. 8:9–14 with him."

Here we read Elder Wing's contemporary, Elder Hibbard, stating the reason Elder Wing had rejected and forsaken the three angels' messages of the Advent movement. The cause?

> "The inconsistency of the old position on the 'daily.'"

Here is documentation that the paganism view caused someone to leave the early remnant church.

We continue with Elder Hibbard's letter to Elder Smith about Elder Wing's experience, as well as his response to Smith's reply, because we can gain fuller understanding about the sanctuary from his reasoning in the letters.

> "He asked, 'what is "the daily" mentioned in these verses?' I replied, 'It is paganism.' When he asked 'What sanctuary is cast down as mention in verse 11?' I replied, 'the sanctuary of paganism.' After this we read verse 13: 'Then

I heard one saint speaking, and another saint said unto that certain saint which spake, How long shall be the vision concerning the daily and the transgression of desolation to give both the sanctuary and host to be trodden under foot?'

"Said he, 'In the vision, what host was to be trodden under foot?' I replied, 'The host of heaven, according to verse 10.' Then he asked, 'What sanctuary, in the vision, has been mentioned as being cast down or trodden under foot?' To this I replied, 'The sanctuary of paganism, according to verse 11.'

"Now after the question asked in verse 13, 'How long shall be the vision concerning the daily, and the transgression of desolation, to give both the sanctuary [of paganism] and the host [of heaven] to be trodden under foot,' the other angel replies, 'Unto two thousand and three hundred days then shall the sanctuary be cleansed.' After reading this, he asked, 'If the sanctuary of the vision was the sanctuary of paganism, and the sanctuary inquired about in verse 13, was the sanctuary of the vision, then what sanctuary is to be cleansed as mentioned in verse 14, since verse 14 is a reply to the question asked in the previous verse?'

"I immediately saw my predicament, and could make no reply at all. He gave me a punch with his finger in the stomach and laughed at me, and that ended the discussion. I, however, told him that I would give the matter thought, for I was sure that verse 14 refers to the cleansing of the heavenly sanctuary, and that the beginning of this even was in 1844.

"The following autumn I began my work in the Battle Creek college as teacher of the Bible; was there three years; but during all that time I could not say a word to any class in reference to 'the daily', because it was not yet clear to me. I spent a year at Walla Walla. Light kept coming; yet I could not see to the end of the matter. I therefore kept quiet. Returning East I connected with the Sanitarium at Battle Creek, was there three and a half years, and yet said nothing about it, tho the Scripture in question had opened before me quite fully. In 1901 I came to Healdsburg as teacher of the Bible; yet even here I kept the matter to myself until it had been made public in a series of Sabbath School lessons written, I believe by Prof. Prescott. I then found out for the first time that there was another individual among us whose mind had been led in the same as my own. Also, about this time, I found that Elders Jones and Waggoner, each studying by himself, had arrived at the same conclusion as Prof. Prescott and myself. This, to me, was encouraging to find that all four of us, without consulting each other, or any human being, had arrived at the same conclusion. But even without this, I should have held to my convictions, because I was persuaded from the Bible alone; not from some finely drawn-out theory, but from the plain reading of the text.

"You are well acquainted with the reading of this Scripture as found in the Revised Versions; and here the reading is so plain that you can not mistake the origin of 'the daily,' nor of 'the sanctuary' of the same;- 'It [the little horn] took away from him [Christ] the daily, and the place of His [Christ's] sanctuary was cast down.' This also agrees with the marginal reading of the King James Version. And even the text of the King James Version itself is not out of harmony with the exact reading which I have referred to. Now it seems to me that no question ought to be asked concerning how this can be, when the plain reading of the Word of God says it is so E. J. HIBBARD (brackets Hibbard's)."

Shortly thereafter, the unpersuaded Elder L. A. Smith replied with a letter and his thirty-two page, two-part tract delineating his paganism interpretation of the "daily" of Daniel 8. E. J. Hibbard responded on November 28, 1909, to Elder L. A. Smith with the following rebuttal:

> "Dear Brother, L. A. Smith
> "I am pleased to get your letter of recent date, also the enclosed leaflet, setting forth your view on the 'daily' of Daniel 8.
> "Assuming now that you have proved your point, then we conclude that the <u>sanctuary</u> of Daniel 8:11 is the <u>sanctuary</u> of paganism. This being true, the sanctuary enquired about in verse 13 is the sanctuary of paganism; and the sanctuary to be cleansed in verse 14 is the sanctuary of paganism. And, of course, in harmony with the questions in verse 13, and the answer in verse 14, when the sanctuary of paganism is cleansed, then the sanctuary of paganism will no longer be trodden under foot by the Papacy.
> "But you do not believe it was the sanctuary of paganism which was to be cleansed beginning in 1844. Neither do I. It was the heavenly sanctuary; and so also is that of verse 11; for the sanctuary of verse 11 is the only sanctuary thus far mentioned in the vision; and verse 13 asks 'How long shall be the <u>vision</u> concerning the "daily" and the transgression of desolation, to give both the sanctuary and the host to be trodden under foot?'
> "Then the reply ('Unto two thousand three hundred days then shall the sanctuary be cleansed') shows that the sanctuary to be cleansed is the same as the one concerning which inquiry was made. Thus: if the sanctuary of verse 14 is the heavenly, and not that of paganism, so also is that of verse 11. No honest person can escape this conclusion." E. J. HIBBARD (emphasis Hibbard's).

We submit this further point of information about the sanctuary. The *miqdash*[4720] (sanctuary) in Daniel 8:11 and the *miqdash*[4720] (sanctuary) in Daniel 9:17 are both designated as the Lord's by Daniel (emphasis below added):

> Dan 9:17 "Now therefore, O our God, hear the prayer of thy servant, and his supplications, and cause thy face to shine upon <u>thy sanctuary</u> (*miqdash*[4720]) that is desolate, for the Lord's sake."

The *miqdash*[4720] (sanctuary) in Daniel 11:31, i.e., "the <u>sanctuary of strength</u>," and the *miqdash*[4720] (sanctuary) in Psalm 96:6 are also one and the same, the Lord's:

> Ps 96:6 "Honour and majesty are before him: <u>strength</u> and beauty are in <u>his sanctuary</u> (*miqdash*[4720])."

Having already witnessed in Daniel 8 that the vision (*chazon*) began in verse one and the only sanctuary brought to view prior to verse thirteen was that of the sanctuary of verse eleven, nothing more needs to be said to show conclusively that the sanctuary of Daniel 8:11 is none other than the sanctuary of Christ.

Another area of misinformation that must be dealt with is Mrs. White's recommendation of Uriah Smith's book *Daniel and the Revelation*. Many feel that she would not have urged the reading of his book if it contained error. Some even believe that her estimation of his writing was that it was inspired. The matter is easily set straight with a detailed statement of Arthur L. White, who at the time was secretary of the Ellen G. White Publications at the General Conference. His statement is entitled *Thoughts on Daniel and the Revelation* (November 1957, reissued May 1966), and here follows:

> "Periodically, inquiry is made as to Mrs. E. G. White's attitude toward

Thoughts on Daniel and the Revelation, some asking if somewhere she has stated or at least implied that it is an inspired book.

"One of Mrs. White's statements that has been thus construed is this: 'The light given was that Thoughts on Daniel and the Revelation [other books named, also—*ed.*] would make their way. They contain the very message the people must have, the special light God had given His people. The angels of God would prepare the way for these books in the hearts of the people.'—E. G. White Letter 43, 1899. (Published in Colporteur Ministry, pp. 123-4.)

"Granting the force of such clear endorsement of the book, it is true that nowhere in Mrs. White's writings, published or unpublished, do we find reference to an angel standing by the side of Uriah Smith while he wrote. And certainly we find no indication that Mrs. White ever considered Thoughts on Daniel and the Revelation to be an inspired book, thus inerrant in all its expositions. The basis for a somewhat widely accepted belief to the contrary is a statement made long after the incident referred to, by one lone early worker, based upon his memory at the time. Here is the statement:

"'Many years ago, when the late Elder Uriah Smith was writing Thoughts on Daniel and the Revelation, while Elder James White and Ellen G. White were at my house in Enosburg, Vermont, they received by mail a roll of printed proof sheets on Thoughts on Daniel and the Revelation that Brother Smith had sent to them. Brother White read portions of these to the company, and expressed much pleasure and satisfaction because they were so concisely and clearly written. Then Sister White stated what she had been shown, as follows:'

"'The Lord is inspiring Brother Smith—leading his mind by His Spirit, and an angel is guiding his hand in writing these Thoughts on Daniel and the Revelation." I was present when these words were spoken.' (Signed) 'A. C. Bourdeau.'

"Memory of One Witness Insufficient

"With all due regard to the sincerity and integrity of the one who made this statement, which some years ago was placed in circulation in printed form, it should be pointed out that in matters of such importance the memory of one witness alone is not sufficient evidence. Moreover, it is demonstrable that in some of the details of the incident, his memory proved faulty. For instance, Uriah Smith's writings on these prophetic books appeared originally in two sections, Thoughts on Revelation being printed first, and Thoughts on Daniel later. At the time Thoughts on Revelation was brought out, Elder and Mrs. White were living in Greenville, Michigan, where Elder White received and commented on the new book. (Review and Herald, July 16, 1867.) As it was a few weeks later that they were in Enosburg, Vermont, it must have been the finished book, not the proof sheets, that formed the basis of the conversation referred to. Moreover, Elder Smith at this time had not even announced his intention to write on Daniel. Therefore, Mrs. White could not have used the exact words attributed to her—'An angel is guiding his hand in writing these Thoughts on Daniel and the Revelation.' As such inaccuracies as these two are found in Brother Bourdeau's statement, the question naturally arises as to whether we ought to count too heavily on the complete accuracy of other minute details of the reminiscent incident.

"Further, even though she spoke commendably of the volume, there are statements penned by Mrs. White which have a negative bearing on the inspiration of Thoughts on Daniel and the Revelation. Speaking, in the nineties, of Elder Smith's books, one of the leaders in our colporteur work asked Mrs. White, 'You believe they are inspired, do you not?' Indicative of her recognition of the folly of the question, she replied, 'You may answer that question, I shall not.'—E. G. White Letter 15, 1895. At another time she was asked a similar question. Here is the question and the answer:

"'Sister White, so you think we must understand the truth for ourselves? Why can we not take the truths that others have gathered together and believe them because they have investigated the subjects, and then we shall be free to go on without the taxing of the powers of the mind in the investigation of all these subjects? Do you not think that these men who have brought out the truth in the past were inspired of God?'

"[Answer.] 'I dare not say they were not led of God, for Christ leads into all truth, but when it comes to inspiration in the fullest sense of the word, I answer, No. I believe that God has given them a work to do, but if they are not fully consecrated to God at all times, they will weave self and their peculiar traits of character into what they are doing, and will put their mold upon the work.'—E. G. White, Review and Herald, March 25, 1890.

With due respect, it is here noted that Uriah Smith's erroneous depiction of Turkey as the king of the north is one evidence of his "mold" on the work. We now continue with Arthur White's recounting:

"Two decades later, in writing regarding an interpretation of prophecy given in Thoughts on Daniel and the Revelation, over which there had arisen some controversy, Mrs. White spoke against 'magnifying the importance of the difference in the views that are held,' and further said:

"'In some of our important books that have been in print for years, and which have brought many to a knowledge of the truth, there may be found matters of minor importance that call for careful study and correction. Let such matters be considered by those regularly appointed to have the oversight of our publications. Let not these brethren, nor our canvassers, nor our ministers magnify these matters in such a way as to lessen the influence of these good soul-saving books.'—E. G. White Manuscript 11, 1910. (Published in Selected Messages, book 1, page 165.)

"And at another time she wrote:

"'There is no excuse for anyone in taking the position that there is no more truth to be revealed, and that all our expositions of Scripture are without an error. The fact that certain doctrines have been held as truth for many years by our people, is not a proof that our ideas are infallible. Age will not make error into truth, and truth can afford to be fair. No True doctrine will lose anything by close investigation.'—Review and Herald, Dec. 20, 1892.

"There stood out clearly, however, in the memory of several workers, the oral expression of Mrs. White that she had seen an angel standing by the side of Elder Uriah Smith as he wrote. While there is no documentary confirmation of this, such would not be inconsistent with utterances of a similar character regarding the work of noble men of God. Thus she wrote of Luther: 'Angels of heaven were by his side, and rays of light from the throne of God revealed the treasures of truth to his understanding.'—The Great Controversy, p. 122.

"And of William Miller, she said: 'God sent His angel to move upon the heart of a farmer who had not believed the Bible, to lead him to search the prophecies. Angels of God repeatedly visited that chosen one, to guide his mind and open to his understanding prophecies which had ever been dark to God's people.'—<u>Early</u> <u>Writings</u>, p. 229.

"However, these expressions have never conveyed the thought of inerrancy in all the positions taken and the various teachings of these men who were mightily used of God. Nor would it be reasonable to assume that words which may have been spoken by Mrs. White as to the presence of an angel, as Uriah Smith wrote, would indicate that he was inspired in his writing, and that he was therefore inerrant in all that he set forth.

"<u>Historical Development of the Book</u>

"The present well-known volume, <u>Thoughts on Daniel and the Revelation</u>, was developed through the decades until it reached its present form." (Underlining and bracketing original.)

From Arthur White's account, we will briefly summarize that development. As previously said, for many years there were two separate books, the first on Revelation and the latter on Daniel. In 1862 James White first got the idea of a complete exposition on Revelation when he attended Uriah Smith's "large and flourishing Bible class." That class had studied Revelation chapter by chapter, reaching consensus on nearly every point. They were "confident that they had found a better harmony than they had before seen, and clearer light on some portions of the book." In their delight, the class decided to repeat their study, one chapter per lesson, and James White seized the opportunity to write and publish in the *Review* the group's weekly study results. The group agreed to study other material if, for some reason, he wasn't able to attend a study session.

On May 17, 1862, the first installment appeared under the title "Thoughts on Revelation." Chapter one was its topic, the material being covered by the quotation of a few verses followed by comments and explanations related to them. Five more chapters were covered in the same manner and published consecutively, until James White left on a speaking tour.

Two months later, the articles were resumed on September 9. But then James White suddenly ended his work on the series. In his coverage of Revelation chapters 8 and 9, he commented only on the first five verses, covering the seventh seal and introducing the seven trumpets. Then, explaining that lack of time would have to excuse him for no further exposition, necessitating his abbreviated coverage, he recommended "as the best light at present" a pamphlet containing Josiah Litch's explanation of the seven trumpets, published by the *Review* in 1859.

Five weeks later, James White reported that since he was away from home much of the time, Uriah Smith had agreed to conclude the series, starting with chapter 10.

Using the same presentation style as James White but writing more extended comment, Uriah Smith continued the work begun by White and covered the remaining chapters month by month, with only one month missed. The series ended on February 3, 1863.

Two years later, *Review* readers learned that its editor, Uriah Smith, was preparing a manuscript for a book to be entitled *Thoughts on the Revelation*. He stated his intention to build upon what he and James White had begun, and he solicited input from readers:

> "We have commenced to revise, and in a great measure rewrite, the 'Thoughts on Revelation,' published in Review, Volumes XX and XXI. We shall devote what time we can to this work, besides preparing matter for the Review, otherwise than writing. If any brethren have any suggestions to make, on any part of the book, we hope to receive them at once."
> *Review and Herald*, July 18, 1865, underlining original.

Uriah Smith also being constrained by other duties from focusing on the book's publication, the book was not ready for sale until June 1867. When reading the completed work, James White wrote:

"These thoughts are not the fruit of one brain. In the time of the end the Revelation was to be unsealed and opened. And from the open book, light has been shining. William Miller saw much. Others since have seen more. This is a book of thoughts, clothed in the author's happy style, plain, yet critical and practical, coming down to the spiritual wants of the common people, yet elevated and dignified. This standard work should be in the library of every believer." *Review and Herald*, July 16, 1867.

The book was revised before the second edition. Five years later, in 1872, the companion book *Thoughts on Daniel* was offered for sale on December 31. It also represented the composite findings of competent students of the Bible. Both books were printed in several editions, and finally in 1881 they were published as the single volume we know today.

Arthur White wrote specifically,

"Elder Smith prepared his manuscripts as a scholarly writer would, setting forth denominational views on the great lines of clearly understood prophecy presented in Daniel and Revelation. But when he undertook the verse-by-verse exposition of these two books, he ran into many texts of Scripture which dealt with matters regarding which we as a people had not given much if any study, and in such cases he often set forth the views of the best commentators available, and used freely both the lines of argument and the words of Josiah Litch, George Storrs, and others. Elder Smith demonstrated remarkably good judgment in the selection of matter from these writers.

"It was but natural that as time advanced, some points became more clear and some errors which had been embodied in his earlier work were seen. This led the author from time to time to make a number of corrections and adjustments in his former statements. Of one such revision, W. C. White wrote in 1910:

"'In 1886, 1887, and 1888 there was considerable controversy over some of the expositions in Thoughts on Daniel and the Revelation. There was quite a group of men, including myself, who became convinced that there were some errors in this most excellent book that ought to be corrected. Elder Uriah Smith defended very ably the positions taken in the book, but he was a very kind and reasonable man, and was willing to make corrections when errors were made plain.

"'Some of Elder Smith's friends and advisers, however, took a very strong position against making any corrections in Thoughts on Daniel and the Revelation. They argued that the book was the result of long, faithful study, that it had received the criticism and approval of the pioneers in our cause; that it had been widely sold and used as an authority by our younger preachers everywhere; that Sister White said that the angel of the Lord stood by Elder Smith as he wrote the book, and that to make changes now would be a confession of weakness and error which would detract from the influence of all our publications and all our preachers; that to make changes would make our ministers ashamed; that we could not longer look the world in the face and say that we had a truth which we could stand by through all the years without vacillation.

"'To this, some of our brethren answered that it was much better to be correct than to be positive; that it was not necessary that we should claim infallibility in our publications in order to secure the respect of the people, and in order that the Spirit of God should witness to the principles which they contain.

"'Some of our ministers and some of our book men argued that if corrections were made, our canvassers would lose confidence in the book, that its sale would be greatly diminished.

"'But finally a number of corrections were made, if I remember correctly about thirty, and the evil results which had been anticipated were never experienced.'—W. C. White Letter to A. F. Harrison, June 26, 1910," underlining in the original.

The book had undergone another, more recent revision at the time Arthur White wrote his account. He concluded,

"As it now comes from the presses we believe it is destined to have a very wide distribution, continuing to fill the important place in our literature which Ellen White said it should have."

She had said interest in it would continue till probation closed.

Thus in this history Arthur White has clarified for us the principle that while men's works—including pioneer writings—are not to be considered infallible, many are nevertheless valuable in their contribution to Scriptural understanding. However, outside of the Spirit of Prophecy, let us not forget our counsel and admonition from the Lord, in matters of faith.

"Let all who accept human authority, the customs of the church, or the traditions of the fathers, take heed to the warning conveyed in the words of Christ, 'In vain they do worship Me, teaching for doctrines the commandments of men.'" *Desire of Ages*, 398.

"We are not to make a study as to what are the opinions of men, what are the traditions of the Fathers, or what is the popular faith. We cannot trust to the voice of the multitude, or follow the world in an evil course. Our inquiry should be, What hath God said?" *Medical Ministry*, May 1, 1892

"We shall be attacked on every point; we shall be tried to the utmost. We do not want to hold our faith simply because it was handed down to us by our fathers. *Such a faith will not stand the terrible test that is before us.*" *Review and Herald*, April 29, 1884.

So what is our only safe and due course?

"But God will have a people upon the earth to maintain the Bible, and the Bible only, as the standard of all doctrines and the basis of all reforms." *Great Controversy*, 595.

# 11

## PAGANISM'S EVER-CHANGING VIEWS

It is now appropriate to address paganism's fourth definition thus far of the "daily." In July 2005 Brother Gerhard Pfandl, associate director of the Biblical Research Institute of the General Conference, addressed this very same issue we have been addressing from another angle. Because of this growing confusion among Seventh-day Adventists, he rebutted a work entitled *The Mystery of "The Daily,"* by John W. Peters (1994). From Brother Pfandl's work, entitled *Evaluation of "The Mystery of 'The Daily'" by John W. Peters*, we will bring to light some of his scholarly work for the benefit of our readers. Along with Brother Pfandl, we have no personal issues with Brother Peters. Our sole purpose is to give our readers the facts needed to draw correct conclusions. The following, we believe, will give confirmation and clarity to the firm foundation that we have already established:

"**Title Page**
"At the bottom of the title page it says: Seventh-day Adventist Theological Seminary, Andrews University, Berrien Springs, Michigan.
"**Comment**: This gives the impression that the document was published by the Theological Seminary. At least, many lay persons will take it that way. Whether this was intended or not, it looks like a deliberate attempt to give the paper an official status. I understand that the Seminary is asking the publishers to remove the reference to the Seminary from the title page.
"**Page 3** [Page numbers refer to pages in Peters' book.]
"'L. R. Conradi in Germany reinterpreted the "daily" as referring to the true sanctuary service and Christ's High Priestly ministry in heaven.'
"**Comment**: Peters gives the impression that

what came to be called 'the new view' began with Conradi. This is historically incorrect. The 'new view' did not originate with Conradi, though he was instrumental in bringing it to the forefront of the debate around the turn of the century.

"**Pages 9–14**

"On the basis of the gender oscillation in Daniel 8:9–12 the author attempts to establish that the power that exalts itself against the Prince of the host in verse 11 is pagan and not papal Rome. The conflict in these verses is seen as a conflict between pagan and papal Rome rather than between the Prince of the host and the papal Rome (the little horn). The following chart is taken from page 14.

v. 9 masc. 'he came' PAGAN
v. 10 fem. 'it became great' PAPAL
v. 11 masc. 'he exalted' 'from him' PAGAN
v. 12 fem 'it cast down' 'it worked' 'it prospered' PAPAL

"**Comment**: Peters relies heavily on this gender oscillation to establish his interpretation. In fact, it is one of the cornerstones of his whole argument. Unfortunately, some of our best interpreters have also relied heavily on the gender identification in verse 9 to establish the point that the little horn came out of one of the four winds, rather than from one of the four horns.

"However, anyone familiar with the Hebrew text knows that gender difference or mixing is very common in the OT. Particularly frequent are the wrong suffixes. Gesenius Kautzsch states: 'Through a weakening in the distinction of gender . . . which probably passed from the colloquial language into that of literature, masculine suffixes (especially in the plural) are not infrequently used to refer to feminine substantives.' (*Gesenius' Hebrew Grammar*, 135 o).

"The same is true in regard to the agreement

between subject and predicate in respect to gender and number. 'As in other languages, so also in Hebrew, the predicate in general conforms to the subject in gender and number. There are, however, numerous exceptions to this fundamental rule. These are due partly to the *constructio ad sensum* (where attention is paid to the meaning rather than the grammatical form), partly to the position of the predicate (regarded as being without gender) before the subject' (*Gesenius' Hebrew Grammar*, 145 a). For example, in Isaiah 49:11 the subject is feminine, but the predicate is masculine: 'I will make all My mountains a road, And My highways (**fem. pl.**) will be raised up (**masc. pl.**).'

"Oscillation between feminine and masculine verbs is also found in other prophetic passages. For example:

"Ezek 23:49 'They shall repay you for your lewdness, and you shall pay (**2 fem. pl.**) for your idolatrous sins. Then you shall know (**2 masc. pl.**) that I am the Lord GOD.'

"Nah 3:15 'There the fire will devour you, The sword will cut you off; It will eat you up like a locust. Make yourself many (**2 masc. s.**) - like the locust! Make yourself many (**2 fem. s.**) – like the swarming locusts!'

"As far as Daniel 8:11 is concerned, various explanations have been suggested. Some of them are: (a) Masculine verb forms are used because there is a tendency in the OT to ignore the feminine; (b) the different genders are indicators of weakness and greatness of the subject; (c) the irregular gender is used intentionally to heighten the reader's attention and to mark specific passages as climax; and (d) the masculine gender refers to the masculine reality behind the feminine symbols used in the text.

"In addition, Martin Proebstle in his forthcoming

Ph.D. dissertation on Daniel 8:9–14 has suggested that the gender in 8:9–12 is used stylistically. That Daniel consciously 'played' with the opposition between masculine and feminine. He points out that there is the following gender balance in verses 9–11.

9a masc.     fem. 9b  
10a fem.     masc. 11a  
10b fem.     masc. 11b  
10c fem.     masc. 11c  

"This arrangement of opposite gender of verbal forms creates a coherence in verses 9–11, he says.

"The point of all this is to show that Peters' foundation is not as solid as he thinks it is. If the difference in gender in Daniel 8 were the only place where it occurs, he would have a point, but since the mixing of genders appears frequently in the OT he cannot use it as the basis of his interpretation. Furthermore, satisfactory explanations can be found for this oscillation, as indicated above, without resorting to the idea that two phases of the little horn are described; something that would escape any reader not familiar with the original Hebrew text.

"In any of the Bible translations, the plain reading of the text describes a battle between the little horn and the Prince of the host, not between two phases of the little horn. Furthermore, in Daniel 7, the parallel chapter to Daniel 8, the issue is clearly between the little horn/Satan and the people of God/Christ, not between two phases of the little horn.

**"Pages 15-16**

"Daniel 8:11 'It magnified itself, even up to the Prince of the host; and the continual burnt offering was taken away from him, and the place of his sanctuary was overthrown' (RSV).

"Seventh-day Adventists generally teach that the little horn (papacy) took the *tamid* (intercessory ministry) away from the Prince of the host (Christ). Peters claims that on the basis of grammatical nearness 'the antecedent of "from him" is the one exalting himself or pagan Rome' (p. 15). After outlining the inverted syntax of verse 11 he concludes, 'This internal reflection of the Hebrew syntax supports the contention that the "daily" is lifted up "from" the one exalting himself and not "from" the Prince of the host' (p. 16). In other words the *tamid* is taken away from pagan Rome and not from Christ.

"**Comment:** The grammatical argument on pages 15 and 16 looks very impressive and convincing, but is it correct? The syntax of verse 11 in Hebrew is as follows (pp = prepositional phrase; s = subject; v = verb):

11a Unto the Prince of the host (pp) he (s) exalted himself (v)

11b and from him (pp) was taken way (v) the continual (s)

11c and thrown down was (v) the place of his sanctuary (s).

"The first two lines begin with the prepositional phrases: 'unto the Prince' and 'from him.' This creates a syntactic-semantic correspondence between 11a and 11b: both clauses start with a prepositional phrase referring to the Prince of the host followed by a Hiphil verb form with the little horn as subject (In the second line the little horn is understood to be the one who takes away the daily).

"As Proebstle has indicated, there are at least two arguments that the pronominal suffix in *mimennu* (from him) refers to the Prince of the host. First, both 'unto the Prince of the host' and 'from him' occupy the preverbal field of their respective clauses. The focus on the Prince of the host established in verse 11a is reaffirmed in verse 11b if the pronominal suffix in *mimennu* (from him) refers to the Prince. There is no apparent reason to switch the focus back to the horn. Indeed, 'from him' is only then natural in the sentence-initial position when it emphasizes the previously mentioned 'Prince of the host', which is also in the sentence-initial position.

"Second, the next clause 11c has no explicit reference to the subject 'horn,' the pronominal third person masculine suffix in 'His sanctuary' also refers to the Prince of the host. According to Peters' interpretation of Daniel 12:9–12 the issue in these verses is not the great controversy between Christ/God's people and Satan/little horn, but a battle between two phases of the little horn – pagan and papal Rome. Christ is only mentioned as an aside in verse 11. This is contrary to the thrust of the whole book of Daniel, which illustrates the great controversy in every chapter."

In other words, 11a and 11b, paraphrased and in parallel construction, read "*to* Jesus the little horn exalted himself, and *from* Jesus the little horn took away the continual." The aggressor is the little horn in all cases, even in the "throwing down" in 11c.

**"Pages 23-30**
"'It is suggested that "the daily" must be carefully defined as a principle, namely the self exalting character of paganism, inherent in mankind, of which Arianism became integrated' (p. 27). Peters attempts to prove this with the following OT texts:
Ps 74:23 'The tumult of those [God's enemies] who rise up against You increases continually [*tamid*].'
Isa 52:5 'Those who rule over them Make them wail,' says the Lord, 'And My name is blasphemed continually [*tamid*] every day.'
Obad 16 'For as ye have drunk upon my holy mountain, so shall all the heathen drink

continually [*tamid*],'
Nah 3:19 'For upon whom has not your wickedness passed continually [*tamid*]?'
Hab 1:17 'Shall they therefore empty their net, And continue [tamid] to slay nations without pity?'
Isa 65:2-3 'A people who provoke Me to anger continually [*tamid*] to My face.'
"Peters argues that in each of these texts the pagan enemies of God in the OT rise up or exalt themselves against God continually (*tamid*). This proves, he claims, that in Daniel 8:11 it is pagan Rome that exalts itself against the Prince of the host and that from him (pagan Rome) the daily was lifted up or taken away by papal Rome (p. 23). He says:
"'The "abomination (transgression) which desolates" in Daniel 8, 11 and 12, which supersedes and replaces "the daily," may be defined as *the self exalting character of nominal Christianity of which the papacy became the fountain head*. The essence of "the daily" is "the mystery of iniquity" which seeks to become like God (Is. 14:12-14; 2 Thess. 2:3-7). The point of commonality between "the daily" and the "abomination which desolates" is the "mystery of iniquity." This character attribute was lifted up by the papal Rome from pagan Rome with the result that the false religious systems (paganism) were replaced or superseded (taken away or turned aside) by nominal Christianity, a new false religious system professing Christ, uncreated, in contrast to Arianism's created Christ. This process commenced in AD 508 when Arian powers under Theodoric made peace with Clovis and the resistance of the Arian powers began to come to an end. (p. 27).'
"**Comment:** This is a rather ingenious way of explaining the word *tamid*. It seems that Peters took the following statement from U. Smith,

'"By him [papal form] the daily [the pagan form] was taken away." Pagan Rome was remodeled into papal Rome' (*Daniel and Revelation*, 1944 ed., p. 161) and tried to find biblical support for this view. However, for the following reasons this explanation is not acceptable:

"1. In each of the texts quoted by Peters the word *tamid* is used as an adverb explaining that an action is going on continually or all the time. There is no indication in any of these texts that *tamid* is a principle of self-exaltation or a character attribute as Peters claims.

"2. The Hebrew word *tamid* occurs 104 times in the OT. 67 times *tamid* is used adverbially (48 times in religious and cultic contexts). 37 times it is used nominally (24 times with the article). Every time the word is used with the article (*hatamid*) it is in a cultic [worship] context.

"3. In the book of Daniel, where *tamid* occurs five times (8:11, 12, 13; 11:31; 12:11) it is always used as an adjectival noun with the Hebrew article – *hatamid*. Since the context in Daniel 8 is also cultic ("sanctuary") *hatamid* should also be understood to have a cultic meaning.

"4. In Daniel 11:31 and 12:11, the *tamid* is replaced by 'the abomination of desolation' (*hashiqqutz meshomem*). The noun *sheqetz* refers to something cultically unclean such as animals prohibited for food (Lev 7:21; 11:10–13, 20, 23, 41–42, etc.), and the noun *shiqutz* refers to abominable idols (1 Kings 11:5; 2 Kings 23:24) and their worship. This is further evidence that the *tamid* refers to a cultic [worship] practice since it is replaced by another, an abominable, cultic practice.

"5. There is no explanation of *hatamid* in the text. This shows that it must have been a well-known term that was easily understood in biblical times. That it must be interpreted against the cultic background of the OT is clear for the following reasons:

"a. *Hatamid* is used 24 times in the OT, 17 times in the Pentateuch (Num 4:7, 16; 28:10, 15, 23, 24, 31; 29:6, 11, 16, 19, 22, 25, 28, 31, 34, 38), twice in Neh 10:34 which refers back to the Pentateuch, and five times in Daniel 8:11, 12, 13; 11:31; 12:11. In the Pentateuch and in Nehemiah it always refers to something in connection with the sanctuary service.

"b. In Daniel 8:11–13 it appears together with several unambiguous cultic terms (*herim* - to remove; *miqdash* - sanctuary; *qodesh* - holy). To deny *hatamid* its cultic meaning in this passage and by extension also in Daniel 11:31 and 12:11 seems contrary to common sense and all the rules of hermeneutics.

"c. In each passage outside of the book of Daniel *hatamid* is the responsibility of the priests. In Daniel, therefore, it seems logical that it also refers to the ministry of the Prince of the host rather than to a characteristic of paganism.

"It is no wonder, therefore, that most Bible translations supply the word sacrifice or similar terms. The context strongly suggests a cultic [worship] meaning for the term *hatamid*.

"**Conclusion**

"Many other points in this 121-page paper could be investigated, but the issue should be clear by now. Peters' view of *hatamid* (the daily) as the self-exalting character of paganism is linguistically and exegetically not sustainable. This paper is a brave attempt to provide exegetical support for what came to be known as the 'old view.' Peters recognized that Uriah Smith's interpretation that the 'the daily' is pagan Rome is contextually not possible; he, therefore, identified 'the daily' with the self-exalting character of paganism, but this too is exegetically and contextually not viable."

With many thanks to Brother Pfandl, we thus conclude the portions we wish to illustrate from his work.

At this juncture we want to expound on a statement of Peters in his book that needs to be addressed. If you recall, the "new view," as we have already documented, is in fact the "old view." Peters wrote,

> "The 'new view' proponents of 'the daily' are unable to exegete this verse [Daniel 11:31], leaving Daniel to self-extinguish in meaningless speculation. Any attempt to suggest that Christ's High Priestly ministry was taken away in 508 either by the institution of penance or the mass cannot be supported." (Pg. 99.)

Peters' claim that we are "unable to exegete this verse, leaving Daniel to self–extinguish in meaningless speculation" has been shown to be totally without substance. We candidly point out, though, that historical documentation to prove the contrary was not in abundance at the time of his written thesis. Now, however, the Bible, Spirit of Prophecy and the records of reliable history, especially some rare primary-source documentation heretofore unknown to Adventism and referenced in this series and in *Source Book*, have systematically torn down every foundation built upon by the proponents of paganism.

> "Let no one come to the conclusion that there is no more truth to be revealed." *Counsel on Sabbath School Work*, 34.

Thus paganism's fourth definition and foundation have been demonstrated to be totally untenable.

There was a time when Ellen White said,

"But let not 'the daily,' or any other subject

that will arouse controversy among brethren, be brought in at this time." *Selected Messages,* 1:167.

Under the circumstances taking place at the turn of the 20th century that we briefly illustrated, the counsel was obviously much needed. Combining those circumstances with "the way this subject has been handled by men on both sides of the question" and understandably:

"At such a time silence is eloquence." Ibid., 168, emphasis added.

This was not for all time, but for "at such a time." The reasoning behind this counsel was clearly given.

"The enemies of the truth, who are watching us closely, will make the most of it, and our work will be hindered." Ibid.

Why did Daniel use two different Hebrew words for "vision"? From the book *Doctrinal Discussions,* published by the Review and Herald, we have a compilation of articles prepared by the Ministerial Association of the General Conference of Seventh-day Adventists, originally appearing in *The Ministry,* June 1960 through July 1961, in answer to Walter R. Martin's book *The Truth About Seventh-day Adventism.* On pages 59–60 of *Doctrinal Discussions,* this very topic is nicely addressed, and the issue is placed in its true light. We include this portion because some have put a false interpretation on the meanings of the two Hebrew words for "vision" and then tried to make more of the differences between the two words than the Bible is actually saying:

"The Tie Between Daniel 8 And Daniel 9
"We have observed that the features of Daniel's prophecy in chapters two and seven were quite fully explained, and that in the main, the features of Daniel 8 were also explained. Only

one symbol was not explained, and that symbol was the 2300 year–day period.

"We maintain that this aspect of the Daniel 8 vision was dealt with in Daniel 9, and we will now consider certain aspects of this question.

*"1. The Significance of the Mention of the Angel Gabriel (Daniel 9:21)*

"The mention of Gabriel we believe is an indication of the tie between chapters 8 and 9. In Daniel 9:21 Gabriel, who comes to make Daniel understand the vision, was the angel Daniel saw in the beginning of the vision as recorded in chapter 8. There Gabriel is counseled by someone of higher authority to give understanding of the vision to Daniel (Dan. 8:16). It was the same angel that was with Daniel when he fainted, and who comforted and assured him that the vision was true. In the seventh chapter there is no mention of Gabriel and no evidence that Gabriel gave that vision to Daniel.

*"2. The Significance of the Expression 'consider the vision' (Daniel 9:23)*

"Gabriel had previously explained to Daniel all but the time portion of the symbolic vision of chapter 8. Now he reappears to continue the explanation in literal terms (Dan. 9:21, 22) and to clarify the remaining part. The angel uses the arresting words 'consider the vision.' This expression provides the key to the explanation, for the term 'vision' appears ten times in chapter 8. But it is to be noted that in Daniel 8 and 9 two Hebrew words, *chazon* and *mar'eh*, not exact synonyms, are used in the original Hebrew text. In the majority of English translations only one word, 'vision,' has been used to express these slightly variant thoughts, and as a result, the exact intent of the original has rarely been perceived.

"Could we not regard the Hebrew words as having some significance? It is possible that when the word *chazon* is used, the reference seems to be to the over-all vision. On the other hand, where the word *mar'eh* is employed, the reference could be to the particular things seen and heard in the *chazon*. One feature seen in the over-all vision, the *chazon*, was the 'two thousand and three hundred days' of Daniel 8:14. But the special scene referred to here is 'the vision' (*mar'eh*) of the evening and morning (verse 26).

"When the angel Gabriel, 'whom I [Daniel] had seen in the vision (*chazon*) at the beginning' (Dan. 9:21), returned to complete his explanation of the vision (*chazon*), he directed Daniel's attention specifically to the vision (*mar'eh*) when he said, 'consider the vision [*mar'eh*]' (verse 23). The very thing, the *mar'eh*, that was unexplained in Daniel 8 is what Gabriel referred to when he said to consider the *mar'eh*.

"'There can be no mistake as to this identification of "the vision." S. R. Driver, the noted critic (*The Book of Daniel*, 1936, p. 133), recognized this and wrote concerning "the vision at the beginning" (Dan. 9:21) that it refers to "viii.16." The chapter 8 usage and the chapter 9 tie-in appears inescapable, and the identical theme of the two chapters becomes self-evident. *What follows in chapter 9 is therefore not a new and independent vision, but is the continuing literal explanation of the symbolic "vision" of chapter 8.'—Questions on Doctrine*, p. 271." (Italics retained.)

Some of you may remember a statement made by F. C. Gilbert that he had had an interview with Ellen White and declared that she saw "papal view agitation" (Gilbert's derogatory term for the ministry of Christ view) to be a "scheme of the devil." I called Tim Poirier at the Ellen G. White Estate and personally asked him if he could verify that Ellen White had indeed said such a thing. After all, to suggest that Ellen White would "in the name of the Lord" call the brethren to come together and study the matter thoroughly, and at the same time declare the "papal view agitation" to be a "scheme of the devil," should cause any honest seeker of truth to see red flags.

If Ellen White really believed the ministry-of-Christ view was a "scheme of the devil," she would have addressed the matter herself, and would have never delegated her responsibilities to secondary sources. How could Ellen White claim it to be a "scheme of the devil," when in fact she herself proclaimed this very same view in *Patriarchs and Prophets*, 357, and *Great Controversy*, 418, that we have viewed already? If the ministry-of-Christ view was indeed a "scheme of the devil," then she just declared her own view to be from the devil. No honest person can escape this conclusion. Then, on the other hand, we have a paganism-biased witness with no other proof than his word. This is by no means the first time the White Estate has encountered just such a circumstance with the same concluding verdict. Tim Poirier gave no credibility to that statement by F. C. Gilbert, and rejected the idea that Ellen White would have said a "scheme of the devil," although he did not offer a definitive substitute. This matter should not be of great concern for the sincere students of the Bible, because we know full well that, in the very near future, misunderstood or fabricated statements like these and more will be said and used against us. Rather, we find our authority and foundation in the scriptures that we have already faithfully built upon.

In conclusion, we will consider one last objection to any study of the "daily." In the past it has been stated that the "daily" is not to be made "a test question." We agree. It has also been said it is not a salvation issue. We agree. And it has further been concluded, "It really doesn't make any difference which view is believed." With that opinion, we are not in accord. We feel that a full and accurate comprehension of the "daily" makes a believer's experience far richer and the sharing of his faith more substantive, more powerful, and more consistent with the three angels' messages and our sanctuary message. Jesus Himself said,

Matthew 4:4 "It is written, Man shall not live by bread alone, but by every word that proceedeth out of the mouth of God."

"Every word." Shall we neglect to investigate and appreciate the understanding God has given us of the significance of this word "daily"?

The disciples' "every word and act was to fasten attention on His name, as possessing that vital power by which sinners may be saved. Their faith was to center in Him who is the source of mercy and power." *Acts of the Apostles*, 28. "Every word" was to fasten attention on Jesus.

"Jesus Christ was the foundation of the whole Jewish economy. He established the sacrificial offerings, which typified himself. The whole system of types and symbols was one compacted prophecy of the gospel, a presentation of Christianity." *Review and Herald*, March 21, 1893.

In addition to other words of great significance, the "daily" focuses on Jesus' ongoing labor on our behalf, and the history connected to the "daily" gives us further understanding.

Is it not significant—does it not thrill the soul—to comprehend that what was "set up" in AD 508 (church and state), was "torn down" on February 15, 1798 by the French civil sword? (See *Source Book*.) God thus initiated the "time of the end," when the prophecies in Daniel's "little book" would be opened to men's understanding. Further, we witnessed that what was "taken away" in 508 (the "daily") was restored after the disappointment of 1844, and what was "cast down" in 508 ("the place of his sanctuary") also was restored, according to Revelation 11:1, as we studied earlier. There is a marked consistency in the prophecies of Daniel, a decided focus to which our attention is being drawn. Shall we not look and see?

The beginning and end of the 1260-year and the 1290-year prophecies centered on a mutual issue—religious liberty. (See *Source Book*.) God's law and Christ's "daily" mediatorial work in the heavenly sanctuary were largely lost sight of—"taken away" from most people's remembrance by a blasphemous system that laid bold claim to heaven's divine prerogative to hear confessions, forgive sin and command obedience. This is confirmed by the following:

> "... *Faith was transferred from Christ, the true foundation, to the pope of Rome.* Instead of trusting in the Son of God for forgiveness of sins and for eternal salvation, the people looked to the pope, and to the priests and prelates to whom he delegated authority. *Thus the minds of the people were turned away [taken away] from God* to fallible, erring, and cruel men, nay, more, to the prince of darkness himself, who exercised his power through them." *Great Controversy*, 55, emphasis supplied.

The Catholic system's centuries of denial of access to the Scriptures under penalty of death prevented many people from reading of the sanctuary work for themselves.

> "Satan well knew that the Holy Scriptures would enable men to discern his deceptions and withstand his power. In order for Satan to maintain his sway over men, and establish the authority of the papal usurper, he must keep them in ignorance of the Scriptures. The Bible would exalt God and place finite men in their true position; therefore its sacred truths must be concealed and suppressed. This logic was adopted by the Roman Church. For hundreds of years the circulation of the Bible was prohibited. The people were forbidden to read it or to have it in their houses, and unprincipled priests and prelates interpreted its teachings to sustain their

pretensions. Thus the pope came to be almost universally acknowledged as the vicegerent of God on each, endowed with authority over church and state.

"The detector of error having been removed, Satan worked according to his will." Ibid., 51.

Through the Protestant Reformation, God returned to true believers the understanding that "the just are saved by faith," not by penitential or beneficent works; the acute awareness of the necessity of "sola scriptura;" and the privilege of appealing directly to Jesus without a human mediator. Yet even the Reformation and the Bible in the common languages had not caused the ministrations in the heavenly sanctuary to return to human memory. In William Miller's time, you recall, earnest students of the Bible knew nothing of a heavenly sanctuary and Jesus' ministry there on their behalf.

What God would have us know, Satan would obscure, remove, or distort.

> "When Adam and his sons began to offer the ceremonial sacrifices ordained by God as a type of the coming Redeemer, Satan discerned in these a symbol of communion between earth and heaven. *During the long centuries that have followed, it has been his constant effort to intercept this communion. Untiringly has he sought to misrepresent God and to misinterpret the rites pointing to the Savior.*" *Lift Him Up*, 26, emphasis added.

It is no wonder, then, why Job said the following of Christ:

> Job 9:33 "Neither is there any daysman betwixt us, that might lay his hand upon us both."

And Ellen White confirms that our continual Daysman is none other than Christ:

> "The I AM is the Daysman between God and humanity, laying His hand upon both. He who is "holy, harmless, undefiled, separate from sinners," is not ashamed to call us brethren. Hebrews 7:26; 2:11. In Christ the family of earth and the family of heaven are bound together."
> *Desire of Ages*, 25–6.

It follows that what Satan has labored to keep from us must be of great significance to us.

Furthermore, it is reasonable to expect that he will also attempt to block knowledge of our High Priest's "yearly" ministration during the antitypical Day of Atonement. For example, evangelical teaching has the atonement accomplished in full at the cross. So does a "social" or ecumenical gospel, which fails to stress the necessity of growth in sanctification. Other churches whose highest goal is an external experience have no need of Christ's heavenly ministry when they think they already have the outpouring of the Holy Spirit. Surely we must seek heavenly wisdom in order to anticipate and discern diversions from truth.

The time period of the 1830s and 40s was the time of the Philadelphia church of Revelation 3. It is before that church that our Lord set "an open door, and no man can shut it." That open door was into the second apartment, the Most Holy Place. But that wasn't revealed until He had purified His church—not once, but three times. The first time came at the first disappointment of March 21, 1843 (Jewish reckoning); believers motivated by fear or caught up in the fervor of the first angel's message dropped away in discouragement or embarrassment, unable to endure the "tarrying time."

The second, in the summer of 1844, was the closing of the popular churches to the message and the faithful either withdrew or were compelled to leave. "Babylon is fallen," said the second angel. True believers had to worship separately from families and friends, and endure ridicule and contempt in order to follow the conviction of their hearts.

The third purification was the Great Disappointment of October 22, 1844. The ranks of Advent believers dropped from at least 50,000 (some estimates are higher) to only fifty—a ratio of a thousand to one.

But not until the weak in faith were sifted out and that small, purified group remained—a scattered band who mistook the event but who were convicted that God had surely led thus far—not until then did our holy God restore the understanding of Jesus' high priestly work in heaven. That incomparable truth was revealed and entrusted to those tested, dedicated saints, and we are their spiritual descendants, entrusted with the same precious understanding. That is no small blessing, and no small privilege and responsibility. Even more, we are recipients of the blessing reserved for those "that waiteth, and cometh to the thousand three hundred and five and thirty days." Daniel 12:12. (See *Source Book*.)

# 12

## MINISTRY VIEW INTEGRAL TO ADVENTISM'S MESSAGE

The understanding of Jesus' high priestly ministration is the unique teaching of Seventh-day Adventism. One cannot overestimate the value of understanding what the "daily" is, and how it was "taken away" until the "time of the end," and how it was then restored to us with the additional understanding of the next and final phase of Christ's sanctuary ministry. It makes our teaching of the sanctuary and the related prophecies plain, consistent, and powerful.

A letter from L. R. Conradi to J. N. Loughborough of April 16, 1907, summarizes the "continual's" relevance to Seventh-day Adventism succinctly:

> "But there is one thing that is continual, and will continue, and that is the true, divine service of God. When, about the year 508, the Roman Catholic Church through the so-called conversion of King Chlodwick [Clovis] of France, received its moral support from kings, and later on, in consequence, from the emperor of Eastern Rome, that church did away with the true sanctuary service of God so completely that its true meaning was entirely lost on the earth. The church established its own sanctuary service, its own priesthood, even professing to continue the Levitical, and establish its own sacrifice in the mass; and to show how completely the knowledge of the true sanctuary service has been done away, we need only to remark that no denomination and no minister and no theologian and no commentary had any more the right idea of the sanctuary service, or any knowledge of the true, divine service in heaven, until, after the 1844 movement, Seventh-day Adventists, in view of

the disappointment, searched in the Bible until the Spirit of God enlightened them, and since that time, the true 'continual' service is being again assigned its proper place.

"We arrive at a consistent, and reasonable explanation, full of harmony, and we arrive at this by comparing Scripture with Scripture.

"I know that different ones have written you about this matter. I do not even question that you are fully convinced that the theory held up to the present time is the right one; but after having read your article, I felt it my duty as a brother to set before you what I believe to be the teaching of the Word of God—an exposition that only strengthens the reasons for our existence as a denomination."

Indeed, our High Priest has now left the first apartment in heaven, where for centuries after His ascension He faithfully administered the "daily" services for us, as we can read in Hebrews. The events of 1844 and beyond, the three angels' messages, the investigative judgment—all reveal a critical development in the plan of salvation. We are now to warn the world that He has begun the final ministrations of the Day of Atonement in the second apartment, explained through the typical "yearly" services on earth. The investigative judgment has begun. The end of human probation is upon us.

Also, a misunderstanding of either the "daily" or the "transgression of desolation" of Daniel 8:13 prevents the comprehension of the verse as having to do with the investigative judgment. That event, in all its fullness, must be understood if our people are to be prepared for it, and must be set forth properly if others are to be warned of it.

What scriptural or historical reasoning can justify the position that the event that began the 1290-year prophecy in AD 508 was the downfall of paganism? Not only will history deny that teaching (which able historians can quickly point out for the world to see, to our discredit and the crippling of our message), but see how it detracts and even diminishes the event that really happened?

It matters not to the enemy of souls what error or substitutionary teaching keeps our thoughts from heaven's on-going activity. This "red herring" teaching of paganism, a mistaken train of thought, serves as well as any device to weaken our teaching and turn minds away from the true focus of the prophecies, so we are less strengthened for what is soon to occur. But we now know of a surety that AD 508 was the start of the "taking away" of the "daily" from Jesus. In his institution of a church-state alliance, Catholic Clovis caused a false mediation to be "set" before mankind in place of the true "daily" ministration.

And what scholarly evidence justifies the viewpoint that the event initiating the 1260-year prophecy in AD 538 is the uprooting of the last of the three horns? To say that a horn (kingdom) has been "plucked up by the roots" (Dan. 7:8) affords no other interpretation but that it has ceased to exist. Both primary and secondary sources reveal that the Ostrogoths lost a major battle in 538 that was indeed a turning point in the war, but it was not the end of the war. Procopius, an eyewitness, shows, and respected historians the world over confirm, that the war continued to go first one way and then the other. The same historical sources declare that after AD 538 the Ostrogoths were a force and foe that Rome battled for nearly two more decades.

In fact, in March of 540 the Persian King Chosroes invaded Roman Mesopotamia, and the Roman General Belisarius was immediately recalled from Italy to Constantinople. By spring of 542 the tide had changed, and on December 17, 546, the Gothic King Totila reconquered Rome. In 547 the Ostrogoths had almost all of Italy back in their possession. Procopius tells us that from AD 536 to 552 Rome was conquered no less than five times. Thus the war alternated and raged on until it finally came to its close in AD 553. (For a factual account of the uprooting of the Ostrogoths taken from primary and secondary sources and its relevance to prophetic history, see *Source Book*.)

Documented history, including an eyewitness primary source, thus destroys the foundation of any teaching about the uprooting of the last three horns by AD 538. For Seventh-day Adventists to perpetuate that insupportable teaching is to expose ourselves to a worldly claim that our faith is based on historical errors! How much more meaningful and critical is the truth that in that year, Rome legally imposed the papal Sabbath upon humanity—with the threat of punishment.

Imagine the scorn and ridicule of the world when it is learned we have not been able to reach consensus on the meaning of the "daily" for well over a century. Does not that confusion and discord diminish the power of God's Word on our lips? Meanwhile, Scripture admonishes us—indeed, pleads with us:

> 1 Cor 1:10 "Now I beseech you, brethren, that ye all speak the same thing, and that there be no divisions among you, that ye be perfectly joined together in the same mind and in the same judgment [will, purpose]."

Shall we continue to ignore that counsel, when our oneness for which Jesus prayed would glorify God?

Furthermore, when accurately informed on historical facts, God's people can more effectively counter attempts to change or reinterpret history to further Rome's power. It is well known that Rome is seeking to cast an entirely new light on the history of her economic, spiritual and political stranglehold in Western Europe during the Dark Ages. She persistently refers to Europe's "Christian heritage," which she wants acknowledged via the European Union. History textbooks have been rendered politically correct or silent regarding Rome's oppressive role in European history. In the United States, efforts to reinterpret the nation's constitutional history with an eye toward uniting church and state reflect a lack of awareness of the reasons European settlers sought her shores in the first place. Shall not our Lord have a people with an accurate historical understanding by which to counter the papal efforts to restore supposedly "Christian roots" in the Old World and, by the image to the beast, to impose the same antichristian principles in the New World?

The correct understanding of what occurred in 508 and 538 relative to the "daily" and God's law gives a solid foundation to our sounding of the second and third angels' messages in these last days. Clovis' fusion of church and state in AD 508 resulted in the abrogation of religious liberty. The parallel to 508 is seen in the second angel's message that Babylon has fallen because "*she made* [compelled] all nations drink of the wine of the wrath of her fornication." The abrogation of religious liberty is yet to be repeated.

Then in AD 538 the Roman Catholic Church, in her first Sunday law since Justinian legislated equality of church canons with state laws (AD 530, Codex I.3.44), subverted God's Sabbath, commanding obedience to the papal sabbath in its stead with the threat of church-determined punishment for non-compliance. The parallel to 538 is the third angel's message that warns us of receiving the mark of the beast (compulsory Sunday worship).

What satanic agencies accomplished before, they will accomplish again in a universal Sunday law. Revelation 17 and 13 reveal quite plainly what is to come in the resurrection of the beast, when the same methods will bring about the formation of the image to the beast.

Surely the malevolent pattern of our enemy is spelled out for all to see—and teach—in the events of prophecy. We can document Rome's *modus operandi* from 508 and 538, and show from current events that "the earth and them that dwell therein" will soon face once again an implacable usurper who will forcibly seek to separate all humanity from their hope that is centered in the heavenly sanctuary. The same cause will produce the same effect.

Thus there is a meaningful, demonstrable consistency in prophecy in which the "daily" figures greatly. Although it is not the only focus in the time of the end, we would be most unwise to consider it a topic of little consequence.

The Antitypical Day of Atonement is at long last upon us. The books of heaven have been opened; the investigative judgment has been in progress since 1844. If we have availed ourselves of the precious services of our heavenly High Priest, if our sins have gone beforehand unto judgment, then we have nothing to fear. Our God is as faithful as His prophecies have been sure.

The End

We invite you to view the complete
selection of titles we publish at:

**www.TEACHServices.com**

scan with your mobile
device to go directly
to our website

Please write or email us your praises, reactions, or
thoughts about this or any other book we publish at:

P.O. Box 954
Ringgold, GA 30736

**Info@TEACHServices.com**

TEACH Services, Inc., titles may be purchased in bulk for
educational, business, fund-raising, or sales promotional use.
For information, please e-mail:

**BulkSales@TEACHServices.com**

Finally if you are interested in seeing
your own book in print, please contact us at

**publishing@TEACHServices.com**

We would be happy to review your manuscript for free.

www.ingramcontent.com/pod-product-compliance
Lightning Source LLC
Chambersburg PA
CBHW070549160426
43199CB00014B/2426